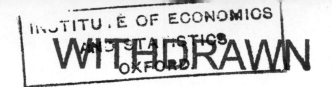
THEORIES
OF THE MIXED ECONOMY

THEORIES
OF
THE MIXED ECONOMY

Edited by
DAVID REISMAN

VOLUME II

ROBERT HALL

The Economic System

in a Socialist State

LONDON
WILLIAM PICKERING
1994

Published by Pickering & Chatto (Publishers) Limited
17 Pall Mall, London, SW1Y 5NB

© Pickering & Chatto (Publishers) Limited
Introduction © David Reisman

British Library Cataloguing in Publication Data
Theories of the Mixed Economy. – Vol. II:
Economic System in a Socialist State. –
New ed
   I. Reisman, David   II. Hall, Robert E.
   330.126
Set ISBN 1 85196 213 1
This volume ISBN 1 85196 215 8

Printed and bound in Great Britain by
Antony Rowe Limited
Chippenham

CONTENTS

ROBERT HALL

Robert Lowe Hall was born on 6 March 1901 in Tenterfield in New South Wales, Australia. His father, Edgar Hall was a mining engineer. Robert Hall was educated in Queensland, first at Ipswich Grammar School and later at the University of Queensland, where he obtained a BEng degree in civil engineering in 1922. (Many years on, it was to be the same university that would award him his sole honorary doctorate, a DSc). In 1923 he came to Magdalen College, Oxford, as a Rhodes Scholar to read for the new degree in Politics, Philosophy and Economics that had admitted its first students in 1921. He received his BA with First Class Honours in 1926.

His special area in the degree was philosophy but he did take three papers in economics. He was presumably still teaching himself the subject when in 1926 he was appointed a Lecturer in Economics, in 1927 a Fellow, at Trinity College, Oxford. He retained his Fellowship until 1950, his Lectureship until 1947. He also held a second Fellowship in Economics, at Nuffield, from 1938 until the effective end of his academic career in 1947.

Market failure was in the air in Oxford in the Depression; and so was the possibility that textbook theory had lost touch with an economic reality of instability and power. On the aggregative side there was the *General Theory* of 1936, with its suggestion that the invisible hand by itself might not be able to price the unemployed back into jobs. In the area of market values both Joan Robinson (in *The Economics of Imperfect Competition*) and E H Chamberlin (in *The Theory of Monopolistic Competition*) had concluded, in 1933, that product differentiation and perceived interdependence necessitated a radical reinterpretation of the behaviour of the firm. The Oxford Economists' Research Group was one manifestation of the search for real-world evidence and improved theoretical explanation that was a characteristic of that era of doubt. Robert Hall was active in the Group from its inception in 1935. He was the author (with C J Hitch) of probably the best known of all the papers it contributed

vii

to the debate on reality at variance with orthodoxy: 'Price Theory and Business Behaviour', published in the *Oxford Economic Papers* in 1939.

The Group when it was constituted in 1935 had decided to rely heavily on the practical experience of businessmen, whom it invited to attend its meetings. Hall and Hitch accordingly proceeded not *a priori* but rather by means of questionnaires and interviews. Acknowledging that a sample of 38 firms (33 of them in manufacturing) is by no means decisive, they inferred nonetheless that the evidence cast doubt on the conventional analysis of the market economy. Businesses, they found, tended to fix prices on the basis not of the marginal cost but of the full average cost (including a standard mark-up for reasonable profits) – and to keep those prices surprisingly stable in the face of temporary (often cyclical) fluctuations in the level of demand. That rigidity they attributed in no small measure to the intrinsic unknowledge of competitors' reactions and oligopolistic strategies that is the theoretical explanation for a 'kinked demand curve' in which it is too great a risk either to cut or to raise a price. Hall and Hitch confirmed the likelihood of a significant shortfall between market potential and market performance that had been postulated by their Oxford colleague, Roy Harrod, in his *The Trade Cycle* (1936). A similar gap between the optimal and the actual had already been considered by Robert Hall himself in his two principal contributions to the theory of the mixed economy: *Earning and Spending* (1934) and The *Economic System in a Socialist State* (1937). A no-nonsense Australian engineer with a solid grounding in philosophy, Hall was determined not to juxtapose ideal types when what was needed was a genuine openness to the market and the State as they really were.

At the outbreak of war in 1939 Hall went into the civil service on a temporary basis. He joined the Raw Materials Department of the Ministry of Supply. After America entered the war he was sent for two years (from 1942–4) to Washington as a member of the British Mission to the Combined Raw Materials Board, which was seeking (without much success) to coordinate the plans of the member countries. Hall gained an insider's insight into public-sector processes. He also got to know the United States.

In 1945 he returned to Trinity College: Anthony Crosland (in 1947 his successor to the Economics Lectureship) was one of his students in this period. Hall continued to work part-time for the

Raw Materials Division (by then integrated into the Board of Trade). A buffer-stocks scheme for staple commodities was one result of his involvement.

James Meade in 1945 had tried unsuccessfully to recruit him for the Economic Section of the Cabinet Office. From 1946 he would presumably have been Meade's deputy. When in 1947 Meade was offered a Professorship at the LSE, Hall was approached to lead the unit, established in 1939 as the first group of professional economists to serve full-time as policy advisors to the Government. Hall accepted and, resigning from Oxford, became Director of the Economic Section, from 1947–53. His *Diaries* (published in two volumes in 1989 and 1991 respectively) give the reader the feel of what he found: 'I inherited a very poor lot from James Meade ... I am trying to screw up courage to tell poor Shackle that we won't want him after his contract runs out – it is painful but he is really no use at all ... Peggy (Hemming), though a first-class economist, is never here.' Of the colleagues whom Hall regarded as better value for money, he was able to retain Marcus Fleming until 1951 and Christopher Dow until 1954, but not Tress, Sayers and A J Brown, all three of whom left with Meade. Hall was successful, on the other hand, in acquiring the services of some of the high-flyers of the future: over the years he managed to hire economists of the stature of B Hopkin, R Neild, M F Scott, A C L Day, W Godley, A Nove and I Little (who in 1950 had taken over the Trinity Lectureship from Crosland and who in 1953 moved on to the Section as deputy to the Director). In 1953 the Section was transferred to the Treasury. Hall was given the title of Economic Advisor to the Government and (in 1954) was knighted. He was succeeded by Sir Alec Cairncross when he retired from the Treasury in 1961 at the age of 60.

Robert Hall served under eight Chancellors in the period from 1947 to 1961. Three were Labour (Dalton, Cripps, Gaitskell), five Conservative (Butler, Macmillan, Thorneycroft, Heathcoat Amory, Selwyn Lloyd): perhaps because of the tolerant centralism of the years of High Butskellism, Sir Robert saw no reason why a political economist known to be a Labour moderate should not be the impartial counsellor of a party that he personally did not support. The period was an eventful one that extended from the post-war fuel shortages and the restoration of convertibility through the Marshall Plan and the 1949 devaluation (strongly favoured by Hall in the face of resistance from the Government and the Treasury alike) to the

Treaty of Rome in 1957, the European Free Trade Association in 1961, the unions' cost-push and the inflationary demand-pull that ultimately led Sir Robert in 1961 to celebrate his retirement with two signed articles in *The Economist* in defence of a national wages policy as the rational alternative to free collective bargaining. While it is never easy to document the precise impact of a single advisor, Sir Robert's influence is generally believed to have been considerable. Good with people, precise and meticulous, his practical, non-theoretical approach to economics was no doubt an asset as well in his day-to-day dealings with Westminster and Whitehall. So was his slight Australian accent, which made him seem classless.

Leaving the civil service in 1961, Robert Hall joined the board of Unilever (until 1971) and became an advisor to Tube Investments (until 1976). From 1963 to 1970 he was Chairman of the Executive Committee of the National Institute of Economic and Social Research: the attachment was eminently fitting in view of the fact that the Institute's *Quarterly Review* had earlier come into being in 1959 as a direct consequence of Sir Robert's wish for there to be an independent check on the Treasury's forecasts. In the 1960s Robert Hall was a part-time economic advisor to the Ministry of Transport. He was for that Department the principal author of *The Transport Needs of Great Britain in the Next Twenty Years* (1963). From 1964–7 he was the Principal of Hertford College, Oxford (and a member of the Franks' Commission of Inquiry into Oxford University). In 1969 he was made a Life Peer as Lord Roberthall. In 1981, joining the new Social Democratic Party, he took the SDP Whip in the House of Lords. Lord Roberthall died on 17 September 1988 at the age of 87.

Robert Hall's scholarly publications principally appeared in the 1930s when he was still an academic. In 1959 there was the *Economic Journal* article entitled 'Reflections on the Practical Application of Economics'. The text of his Presidential Address to the Royal Economic Society, the 55 paragraphs meticulously numbered as if in a civil service brief, it reveals a useful economist's concern about a discipline steadily retreating from reality into abstraction: 'If I may make a personal confession', Hall wrote in his 1959 paper, 'I am frequently struck by how much value I get from my academic colleagues in oral discussion as compared with what I learn from their writings. Indeed, much of the profession seems to exist in a state of controlled schizophrenia – once paper is on the table, good sense and a sense of proportion seem to fly out of the window'. Four years before that, in 1955, the *Oxford Economic Papers* published 'The Place of the Economist in Government' (the Sidney Ball Lecture which Robert Hall delivered in Oxford in 1954, 30 years on from Keynes's celebrated Ball Lecture of 1924 on 'The End of Laissez Faire'). In that lecture the Economic Advisor drew attention to the extensive economic involvement of the modern government ('Today it has a finger in every pie, and often both hands'). He argued that those responsibilities must in turn mean the use of professional guides, aware of interdependencies and able to think analytically. For the most part, however, Robert Hall's scholarly reputation is bound up with the 1930s – with 'Price Theory and Business Behaviour' and with the two book-length contributions to the programmatic science of political economy.

Earning and Spending (1934) was published in the Standpoints series that had been initiated by the Reverend K E Kirk (Regius Professor of Moral and Pastoral Theology at Oxford) in order to promote 'genuinely Christian ethics' through intellectual debate. The book grew out of a lecture on morality and choice that Hall (himself an agnostic) had given at the invitation of Kirk and that appeared in Kirk's *Personal Ethics*, also of 1934. Hall's theme was the wisdom of the Invisible Hand that had sensibly made the profit-seeking capitalist the servant of his neighbour's utility and of his nation's best interest. Hall's *caveat* was the Pigovian spillover that sometimes forced the State to intervene to make education compulsory or to block off contagious diseases. Hall's personal ethics was evidently bound up with individual autonomy and tolerant acceptance. Even where he envisaged that the State would take a lead, the justification that Hall provided for the apparent paternalism was the citizen's satisfaction *ex post* with the drainage scheme or the regulation of gambling that *ex ante* the individual had never expected to prove so advantageous.

The Economic System in a Socialist State (1937) is on the surface an unexpected sequel to the eulogy of the successful businessman as a public benefactor: whereas in 1934 Hall had concentrated on the part, the focus in 1937 was most clearly the whole. The differences are, as it happens, by no means as great as the shift in emphasis from market to plan would seem to suggest. With respect to the market, Hall on capitalism was ever the realist: insistent that private vices need not be public virtues in the case of the natural monopoly or the restrictive union, aware that public goods like effective sewers and countercyclical policies like monetary regulation presuppose an active State, Hall took the view that real-world capitalism was significantly closer to the middle ground than the idealisation of the ideologues would appear to suggest. With respect to the economic plan, Hall on socialism was no less a pragmatist and a theorist of the middle way. Hall did not devote much attention to the case for and against the nationalisation of the productive base. What he did do (in the shadow of Hayek's *Collectivist Economic Planning* and Barbara Wootton's *Plan or No Plan*) was to sketch out an economic framework for welfare and efficiency in a socialist system that involves the State. Market-clearing prices should be the channel through which consumers' valuations exercise their impact upon suppliers' decisions. Firms should expand if they can earn a surplus above cost and (always allowing for a genuine externality that warrants a subsidy) should be closed if they cannot. Rent and interest (uneconomically suppressed in the Soviet Union) should be relied upon to ration scarce land and capital. Wage-differentials should be respected as incentives even by equalisers who attack as non-functional the skewed distribution of inherited property. Socialist management should be promised operational independence (the model of the London Passenger Transport Board) and not be constrained, like the Post Office of the 1930s, by ongoing ministerial interference. Good games presuppose good rules. *The Economic System in a Socialist State* is not a *plaidoyer* for the choice of the socialist game. Rather, it is a set of economic rules intended to ensure that the choice of the socialist game should move the society in the direction of perceived well-being and not condemn it to the purgatory of waste.

FURTHER READING

Primary

(and Hitch, C J), 'Price Theory and Business Behaviour' (1939), in Wilson, T and Andrews, P W S, eds., *Oxford Studies in the Price Mechanism* (Oxford: Clarendon Press, 1951)
'The Place of the Economist in Government', *Oxford Economic Papers*, Vol. 7, 1955

'Britain's Economic Policy', *The Economist*, Vol. 200, 16 and 23 September 1961

Secondary

Cairncross, A K, Preface to Roberthall, R L, *The Robert Hall Diaries 1947–53*, ed. by A K Cairncross (London: Unwin Hyman, 1989)
Jones, K, *An Economist among Mandarins: A Biography of Robert Hall* (Cambridge: Cambridge University Press, 1994)

THE ECONOMIC SYSTEM IN A SOCIALIST STATE

THE ECONOMIC SYSTEM

IN

A SOCIALIST STATE

BY

R. L. HALL

FELLOW OF TRINITY COLLEGE, OXFORD

MACMILLAN AND CO., LIMITED
ST. MARTIN'S STREET, LONDON
1937

PREFACE

THE idea of Socialism is not a new one, but the name is barely a hundred years old and the modern Socialist movement has its roots not much further back. Early writers on the subject paid little attention to the problems of organisation in the Socialist state. But in the present century the Socialist movement reached the point where serious attempts to set up Socialist communities began to be possible, and in 1917 Russia initiated the first experiment of importance. By this time the problem of organisation had begun to be studied, chiefly under the stimulus of criticism from non-Socialist writers.[1]

Broadly speaking, the problems of Socialism from the economic point of view can be divided into two: the theoretical and the practical. The theoretical one, which is the subject of the present book, is the problem of choice between alternative uses of the limited resources by means of which we satisfy our economic needs. This can be formulated so as to be amenable

[1] See on this point Professor von Hayek's Introduction to *Collectivist Economic Planning*.

to treatment on the lines developed by the mathematical economists: Pareto considered that the solution was essentially the same for an enlightened Socialist régime as for a competitive one, and Barone gives a solution.[1] Professor Frisch [2] seems to think that the mathematical method can be applied directly to actual affairs, but no-one else supposes that much progress could be made in this direction in any régime. The method shows us the conditions which have to be satisfied, but does not in itself indicate the way in which this can be done. There have been several attempts to apply economic principles to the problem in a descriptive as well as an analytical sense, such as those of Mrs. Wootton,[3] H. D. Dickinson,[4] and W. Crosby Roper.[5] (A convenient bibliography of the subject is given by Professor Hayek.[6]) These have all the essential similarity which may be expected from the use of a common tradition of analysis, which is applied in this book also, in a somewhat more detailed form, it is hoped, than in previous works in

[1] Reprinted as an appendix to *Collectivist Economic Planning*.

[2] *Econometrica*, vol. ii. Nos. 3 and 4.

[3] *Plan or No Plan*.

[4] "Price Formation in a Socialist Community", *Economic Journal*, June 1933.

[5] *The Problem of Pricing in a Socialist State*.

[6] *Op. cit.*

English. There is clearly room for a fuller investigation of the subject, and contributions which turn out to have no positive value may yet be useful in indicating dangers to be avoided. On the other side, a number of writers have argued that a Socialist state cannot have an economic structure which will enable it to make rational choices, either for reasons which are considered in Chapter V, or because the lack of the profit motive will result in the stultification of the mechanism from lack of driving force. Objections under the latter head are practical rather than theoretical, and it is doubtful whether valid deductive arguments can be drawn in this field: if the arguments are meant to be inductive, there is still some lack of cases.

The practical problem is nevertheless of great importance. And as no attempt is made in this book to consider it, a warning should be given that there is no necessary connection between schemes on paper and those which may actually be put into operation. A Socialist state might very well fail to set up a mechanism which allows it to make rational choices: the Russian system began with nothing of this sort and reasons are given in the Appendix for supposing that it is still some way from an adequate pricing mechanism. If we are to trust to experience, it must be admitted that few states have been happy in their economic experiments, though we have made some progress since Adam Smith recorded his belief that "the statesman who should attempt to direct private people in what manner they ought to employ their capitals . . . would assume an authority . . . which would nowhere be so dangerous as in the hands of a man who had folly and presumption enough to fancy himself fit to exercise it".

It may be argued that some simpler form of direction would be adequate; that a rough method of choice would give a rude plenty which is all that is really wanted by the average man. This view is rejected in the body of the book for reasons given there. But even if a Socialist state established an adequate mechanism through which it could ascertain its relative errors, of over-production of one good at the expense of under-production of another, it might still be unable to enforce productive methods which would give it absolutely sufficient quantities of all goods.

The advantage of the modern capitalist state is that it is highly efficient in the technical sense, being capable of producing large quantities of goods from its resources. This is shown in a striking manner by the severe economic maladjustments which it can endure with little real inconvenience. No state with inefficient technical methods could afford the luxuries of large-scale unemployment, of rigid limitation of production and trade, and of actual destruction of goods already produced: yet these are almost commonplace features of the present depression, during which there has been nothing approaching famine conditions in England or in America. Though we may be dissatisfied with the standards of the poorer sections of the community to-day, these compare favourably with those of the average individual in many periods of history.

It is self-evident that there can be no theoretical answer to the problem of efficiency if it is really a practical one, depending for data on experimental material not yet available. The present book does not attempt any answer, nor could any work which used the same methods. It is indeed unlikely that there could be a reasonable operation of the mechanism here considered and at the same time gross technical inefficiency, but it is perfectly possible that a state should attempt to apply these methods and do it very incompetently or badly. It is also possible that technical efficiency might be combined with a much rougher solution of the economic problems, and that the population might be satisfied with the result.

But in the absence of technical efficiency the price of equality would be a reduction of the common standard: the most easily achieved equality is that of a common misery. It is much to be hoped that it will be possible to estimate the technical success of the Russian system in the near future: reasons are given in the appendix for doubting whether it is one which gives economic efficiency. At the same time, the failure or the success of the Russian experiment will not be clear proof of the necessary practical failure or success of any Socialist experiment: neither men nor societies are sufficiently similar to allow of generalisation from one example.

In the opinion of the writer, few Socialists have grasped the complexity of the modern economic structure, which functions so unobtrusively that it is easy to take for granted the interrelations of its parts, and to assume that we shall retain our present co-ordination in a new economic order without the deliberate organisation of an alternative system. It is the duty of all who advocate a change to acquaint themselves with the probable implications of that change. Socialism will not be easy to achieve, but the pains of transition, if transition ever comes, will be less where they have been foreseen.

PREFACE

This book is based on lectures given in Oxford in Hilary Term, 1934. The subject has been discussed freely among economists in recent years and it is difficult to know and hence to acknowledge obligations. I hope that I have referred either in the preface or in the text to the published material which I have found most relevant.

I am much obliged to my wife, who has read and criticised the work at every stage.

CONTENTS

CHAPTER I

THE ECONOMIC SYSTEM IN A SOCIALIST STATE

xiv

CONTENTS

CHAPTER XI

CHAPTER XII

THE ECONOMIC PROBLEM

THERE is general disagreement as to what is the end or purpose of life: this is not surprising in view of the absence of any objective criterion by which content can be given to the words. Anyone who proposes to lay down rules, whether for individuals or for societies, must choose between his own opinions and those of others, and at most can hope to command assent for limited fields and periods, since there cannot be any universality about propositions involving purpose. There is no such thing as a rational course of action and the word rational should only be used of actions with respect to a stated end, in which there is no contradiction. If I want to reach a certain place in the shortest possible time, it is rational to choose the quickest means of conveyance; but it is improper to say that my desire to be there is rational unless I wish to reach that place as part of some wider given plan which it is my intention to carry out.

Observation shows us that most men require

various adjuncts in order to attain whatever ends they happen to set before themselves. The most obvious of these are food and shelter, which are required by everyone in order to remain alive to carry out any further activity. Extremely few men are content with the necessary minimum of these; the great majority seek to obtain quantities of them and of objects which will afford them the means of entertainment or distraction: of knowledge, and so on. Those means towards human ends which are exchangeable in measurable quantities form the subject-matter of economics, and in a modern community they comprise everything which can be bought and sold. Most men, if questioned, would agree that their opportunities for attaining their ends, whatever they are, are much restricted by the difficulties which they find in obtaining such things: although it is probable that modern civilisations are less restricted in this manner than most of those which have gone before.

This scarcity of material, of exchangeable goods and services, constitutes what is called the economic problem and arises from the disparity between our wants and our means of satisfying them.[1] All economic goods come from

[1] For a discussion of this matter see Robbins, *The Nature and Significance of Economic Science.*

2

the earth or from human labour, and in most cases from a combination of labour and natural products; while the labour is generally assisted by goods previously made, which are called capital. There is not enough of the products of the earth to satisfy everyone: the time during which men can work is small compared with their desire for the results of their labour, and the capital which we have accumulated is insufficient for us. In short, the means of producing goods are scarce, and hence also the goods themselves.

This involves a problem of choice; we can put the land and capital to alternative uses and work towards a variety of products, and every decision means that each of the other possible uses must be renounced. All choices or decisions of this kind are economic ones, and the economic problem includes the field of such decisions. For an individual, the decisions to be made are how to dispose of his labour and his property (if he has any) in order to give himself an income; and how to spend his income, among the large number of possible ways open to him, in that particular one of them which shall be most conducive to his own ends, some of which, as we have said, are likely to involve for their attainment the disposal of economic goods. Only if he has a sufficiently

3

large income to be able to attain without calculation all those goods which he needs, can he be said to have no economic problem. This case arises chiefly for those men with ends involving few scarce goods or services of an exchangeable kind: such as those who wish to lead a life of religious contemplation, or of research which involves few instruments, or of sitting in the sun; if these people can obtain enough income to keep themselves in health and do not have any other ends, they have only to choose between different uses of their time. And if they are able to devote all that is not needed for sleeping and eating to a single purpose, they have no problem at all. Very rich men might also have no problem except the disposal of their time, if they had restricted tastes and no desire to increase their incomes. Obviously members of these classes are few in number and can only exist because others make available the goods which they use.

For most of mankind the problem of scarcity remains. It is comparatively simple for the individual, but it is apparent that the economic structure in which he finds himself determines to a large extent the results which will follow from the choices which he makes. We can only employ our labour and our property in the ways available to us, and we can only spend our incomes on the goods which are for sale at the prices which we find ruling. For society as a whole the problem is an extensive one and can be subdivided into several heads.

It must somehow be decided—

(a) What kinds of goods and services to produce.

(b) By what methods they are to be produced.

(c) The relative proportions in which they are to be produced.

(d) The shares which each individual is to have of what is produced.

Unless we include leisure as a scarce good, there is also—

(e) The length of time which each person is to work. Finally, it must be decided—

(f) How much to save.

In most communities, savings in the form of capital facilitate the processes of production and thus increase the amount produced and available for consumption. But it is obvious that while they are being accumulated they reduce the amount that can be consumed currently. If I buy a motor-car I can have more transport in the future, but while I am saving money for this purchase I cannot spend the amount on other kinds of goods which would have been conducive to present satisfactions. When I say that I cannot afford a car, I mean (if I refer to the capital outlay) that I consider it more important to keep up my other spendings (such as amounts spent on rent and food) than to contract them in order to accumulate funds.

These decisions will determine the nature and quantities of scarce goods available for each individual, and thus his economic position. This will not, of course, determine the ends which he will attain; for example, whether he will be happy or healthy or attain salvation. But if he is able to understand the connection between means and ends, an improvement in his economic position should be of assistance towards his other purposes, and most men do in fact desire to improve this position. It may be argued, therefore, that it is in some sense rational to try to make these decisions in such a way that the goods available are as plentiful as possible.

There is little agreement about the answers to questions (d) and (e). The subject of this book is the question as to whether a rational method can be found to answer all the questions except (d) if a society decides on a particular kind of answer to this question; that is, when it is decided to attempt to distribute the income more or less equally between each

6

individual. It is impossible to answer the first three questions at all until some decision has been taken about the distribution of incomes, for we shall see that the types of products and the quantities of each kind cannot be settled rationally unless we know the proportions each is to get.

The difficulty of the problem for any sort of society comes from the large variety of possible answers that may be given, since, as has been said, each one shuts us off from all the others. It is therefore not soluble by any simple means such as is sometimes thought to be possible by the use of the exact sciences. It sometimes appears that the correct answer is to produce everything as efficiently as possible in the engineering sense, but this begs at least two questions—what is meant by everything and what is meant by efficient.[1]

If we have decided how much to give each person or adopted some mechanism (such as the institutions of property and free contract) which will allow this point to settle itself, there are in general three possible ways of proceeding. These are as follows:

(1) To settle in some arbitrary way the kind of things people are to have: this is a form of rationing. Thus if a Pharaoh should decide to

[1] See Robbins, *op. cit.*, pp. 31-35.

set his people to the work of building pyramids there could be a comparatively simple economic system, since they would have to produce whatever was necessary to keep themselves efficient and the remainder of their resources could be devoted to the work of construction. This kind of answer would be that arrived at by a community whose members pursued military conquest or research in higher mathematics, to take widely different examples.

(2) The individuals could be asked what they considered advantageous for their ends. The only satisfactory way of doing this is through a system of prices: economic systems which have the institution of free exchange are examples of this.

(3) A study might be made of the nature and characteristics of man, and from this his needs might be deduced and the appropriate goods supplied. For example, almost all men wish to avoid infectious diseases, but as they do not know how to attain this end it is usually done for them by some Government agency.

Most countries present a mixture of all these methods in varying degrees; and as there is also some diversity in the methods of settling incomes, we find that there is great complexity of economic conditions in the world. For reasons to be considered in more detail later, there is almost always a considerable amount of individual choice through a price system: this is combined with more or less of the other two methods, which are difficult to distinguish from one another owing to the difficulty of knowing whether the economic activities of Governments do in fact serve the ends of the community, as they are invariably represented to do. A study of history suggests that there is usually a mixture of both, as well in democracies as in those states in which political power is in the hands of some smaller section of the community.

It should be clear that economics is a science, or perhaps it would be safer to say a branch of knowledge, which does not deal with ends in themselves, and that it confines itself to the discussion of the problem of how to reconcile some given system of ends with the scarcity of means through which it is hoped to achieve them. And in particular, it has to be given as data the distribution of incomes and the ends which are to be served. It is possible, however, if these are given, and also the available quantities of resources and the state of technical knowledge, to demonstrate that one particular set of answers to our questions (a), (b), and (c) is more economical, in a sense to be defined, than any other, and it seems therefore that this would be the rational economic system in the stated circumstances. It is also possible to make some comparison of the probable results of different systems of organisation of income distribution, with respect to the average and median quantities of goods made available. Any estimate as to the results achievable with these quantities, which would enable us to say that one system is likely to be better than another, is unfortunately impossible: the comparison of ends must remain a matter of opinion.

CHAPTER II

THE COMPETITIVE SOLUTION

THE solution of the economic problem with which we are most familiar is that which is based on the institutions of free contract and the private ownership of property, and is called the competitive solution. It is discussed at length in works on Economic Theory, partly because it provides a convenient basis of comparison when considering the events which actually happen; and partly because most societies still have their economic arrangements determined by this system, modified in various ways. A short summary of the working of a competitive system will serve as an introduction to many of the problems which all systems, including the Socialist one, are likely to encounter, and will illustrate the concept of a rational adjustment of means to ends. The central problem is the same: it is the income distribution which is different.

The essentials of free competition are that everyone shall be allowed to use or to exchange whatever he possesses of economic significance

11

(whether goods or resources capable of producing them) in any way he pleases; and that no-one takes account in his transactions of the immediate effect that these have on the rates at which he can carry them out. The first condition means that there is no imposition of a co-ordinated scheme upon the individual: the order which is obtained is an incidental result of the behaviour chosen by each member of the society. The second condition means that no-one acts as a monopolist (or oligopolist): whether he controls an appreciable part of the supply of anything or not, he acts as if his own supply were too small a part of the whole amount to have an appreciable effect on the price.

It is a commonplace that everyone does better for himself if he specialises, concentrating on the production of some particular commodity rather than attempting himself to satisfy his own wants directly; and exchanging his own products for the results of the efforts of others. The total result is very much greater as a result of this specialisation; but in the competitive society no-one arranges a scheme of work for the community as a whole, while in the Socialist state there is a central body which does the work of co-ordinating.

Thus, in a competitive society the producers

have to make their own exchanges, and to do this some form of money is required. The essential characteristic of this is that everyone should agree to use it; let us assume also (for purposes of exposition) that the quantity of it is fixed, that it is perfectly durable and can be divided into small fractions, and that it is no use for anything but a medium of exchange. Then everything is exchangeable into money and *vice versa*: and the amount of money offered for a good (or service) is its price. Further, let us assume that everyone uses all the money which he receives at any time evenly over the period which elapses before he receives a further supply.

In modern societies the unit of production is usually a fairly large one, and the process is controlled by an individual whom it is usual to call the entrepreneur: he may be the owner or the managing director. He employs the labourers and other factors of production and sells the finished goods; not because he has agreed with them to co-operate, but because he can offer them more for their services than they could obtain if they worked by themselves. Incomes, then, arise from payments from the consumers to the entrepreneurs, and from the payments from the latter to the owners of the factors of production in the form of wages,

13

dividends, etc. What remains to the entrepreneurs forms their own income. Since all incomes are spent, the total spent by entrepreneurs and owners of factors of production together must equal the amounts received from the sales of goods over any period; there is always enough money to buy the goods if the receipts from their sale are spent.

In order to receive incomes, the entrepreneurs must produce goods which will be sold and the owners of the factors of production get their resources employed by the entrepreneurs. Individual consumers will buy those goods which they consider most conducive to the satisfaction of their own needs or service of their own ends. In order to make the most satisfactory use of income, it must be spent so that the last unit (say a shilling) of it spent on any one commodity shall be as conducive towards our ends as the last shilling spent on any other commodity. This proposition, which sometimes seems strange to those who encounter it for the first time, follows immediately if we are in fact attempting to satisfy our most urgent wants: for if a shilling spent on oranges gives me more satisfaction than a shilling spent on cigarettes, it is rational to reduce the expenditure on cigarettes and increase that on oranges. It is no more than a matter of definition of how we behave, on the supposition that it is empirically true that we try to improve our situation with respect to scarce goods.

Now it is true of almost all commodities that the less we have of them the more we want units of them, and that the more we have the less do we want further units. On the other hand, the higher the price of anything the more must be foregone of other things in order to secure it, and *vice versa*. Hence, by varying the price, any demands on the part of the consumers can be adapted to any supply, for an increase in price restricts the amount that will be bought and a decrease in price increases it. Exceptions to this rule are unimportant for all practical purposes.

Whatever the prices, the consumers' outlays will always be adjusted so that they cannot improve their positions with the existing incomes and supplies of goods. Those who want the goods most intensely, as measured by their willingness to pay and thus to sacrifice other possible goods, will obtain them; the scarce goods go to satisfy the most intense monetary demands. Anybody can put himself in the same position as anyone else with the same income, since if he prefers to do so he can buy what the other person is buying instead of his own purchases; thus he can place himself, if he chooses, in the position most satisfactory to himself with respect to the goods, and presumably he endeavours to do so. When this point is reached the prices of the goods will not change until either the consumers' tastes or the supplies of goods alter. And no-one's position can be improved without damaging someone else's, since to give anyone more will be to force someone else to take less.

The entrepreneurs purchase the services of the factors of production and set them to work making those goods which they hope to sell for a price as much above the cost of these factors as possible: the difference is their profit and provides their income. If the price does not cover the cost they abandon production, since losses are made instead of profits; as the output is reduced, the goods get scarcer and the price can be raised; this will continue until the price has risen at least to the level of the cost. But if the price is well above the cost, the entrepreneurs (since they are neglecting the effect of individual operations on the price) will hire more factors and increase the output, while those who are producing other and less remunerative goods will be tempted to invade the more profitable field; the price must be lowered as the output increases. As the prices change, the consumers buy less of the goods with rising prices and more of those with falling prices, always adapting expenditure to give the most satisfactory set of purchases.

If all the entrepreneurs have equal ability, this process will end when profits are at the same level in each type of production. If they have different abilities, the position is more complicated.

In general, it will be possible to establish plants or factories or other forms of productive unit which have different average costs of production. And those entrepreneurs whose plants are more efficient will make higher profits than their competitors and will expand their output by establishing new plants. This will reduce the price of the product, and may increase the costs of the factors of production, because in most cases more must be paid for each if the increased demand is to be satisfied. But if each entrepreneur acts as if his own output were too small to have an appreciable effect on the price, this process will continue until everything is produced by the most efficient of the available ways, and is being sold at this, the minimum cost of production possible with the existing state of knowledge. For if different entrepreneurs have different efficiencies, the ones with the lower costs will find it profitable

17

to expand with new plants similar to their existing ones until they have supplanted all their competitors who are unable to imitate their methods.

But if the entrepreneurs find that for any reason (such as the difficulty of controlling many plants as efficiently as a smaller number) their attempts to expand cause their costs to rise, they will stop the process of expansion when the cost of the last unit produced, the marginal cost, is just covered by the price. And the effect of competition will then not reduce the price to the lowest possible cost of production, for men of ability are too scarce to produce all that is required at this cost; and the consumers must pay enough to cover the costs of the less efficient, who are still necessary to supply the whole amount which the consumers will pay for.

Thus competition gives those products to the community which they are prepared to pay for; which they want most, in fact. And they get them at the lowest costs at which the last units which they want can be produced. The profits remaining to the most efficient of the producers are due to their superior abilities, but if they were dispensed with, the community would be worse off, for their place would have to be taken by men even less

18

efficient than those whose costs are only just covered by the price. The costs *and* the profits of the more efficient are less than the costs alone of the less efficient. This result has been brought about not because the producers have any philanthropic desire to give the consumers what they want as cheaply as possible, but because the producers are trying to make their own incomes as large as possible. Competition acts as a sort of natural selection.

So far, we have taken the costs for granted. These are determined by two conditions: the demand of the entrepreneurs who wish to employ the factors of production in order to sell goods and thus make themselves incomes, and the supply of the owners of the factors of production who also wish for incomes. Some processes will be of such a kind that they require fixed proportions of the raw material, labour, and capital, and these must be bought at the market prices, determined by the general relations of supply and demand; in full equilibrium the products will be sold at the cost of these factors. Such processes are said to be technically determined and would exist either where only one way of producing a product were known, as might happen in backward communities (whose economic systems, however, are unlikely to resemble at all closely the

19

one we are discussing), or where one process was so superior to all the others possible within a wide range of cost that none of these could compete with it.

Cases of this kind are most unusual: sometimes a fixed quantity of raw material is required to make a product, as when a certain size of uncut diamond is necessary to make another size of cut one; even here there are probably various ways of extracting diamonds. In the majority of cases, various processes are possible and the entrepreneurs endeavour to choose the cheapest combination of factors which will satisfy the demand. To do this it is necessary to make experiments, and in particular to try to isolate the contribution made by each factor of production in order to discover whether: (*a*) it is costing more or less than is brought in by the product which can be attributed to it; (*b*) some cheaper factor can be substituted for it.[1]

---

[1] This question will need fuller discussion later. In the writer's opinion, there are always sufficient cases in a competitive society where it is possible to isolate the contribution which is made by each factor of production, for marginal productivity to be calculated. In other cases entrepreneurs must pay a sum equal to the value of this for similar factors. Their demand is a joint one and the only condition they must satisfy is that their total costs should equal their receipts. Their demand, of course, is part of the total demand for factors and helps to determine the price of them.

If the products of factors of production can be calculated, it will pay the entrepreneurs to employ each one up to the point where the value of its product is just equal to its price. If the employer takes the rest of his factors of production as given, and calculates the effect on the output of adding successive amounts of any one factor, he will find that the difference in output for each unit will first rise and then fall; this must be true for all factors, since additional units find less and less occupation as the other factors become, so to speak, saturated with them; for example, extra amounts of fertiliser to a field, or extra drivers to a train or railway system. Thus, for any factor a price will be possible at which it will pay to employ it, and factors in general must choose just those prices at which they will all be employed: each will then get the amount of product which it would produce if it were employed on the margin.

Similar units of a factor of production must receive the same return in equilibrium, wherever they are employed;[1] since the owner of each is free to contract with any employer he pleases, it will pay anyone receiving less than another to re-contract with the employer who is paying

[1] This implies either that there are no obstacles to mobility or that these obstacles constitute a dissimilarity for otherwise similar factors.

21

more, and it will pay this employer to engage him. If two factors have different produc-tivities they will naturally be paid different amounts: thus we should expect great varia-tions in the payments to labour owing to the different abilities of different men. The general principle is always the same: if you produce what is scarce, you receive more than if you produce what is less scarce, scarcity being interpreted in relation to monetary demand. The best film actor receives more than the best chess player; though each is unique in the sense that there is only one of him, they are comparable because both will be paid according to their want-satisfying capacity.

The extreme case of differences in capacity is to be found with land; for most purposes a good deal of land is needed, *e.g.* for wheat-growing, but there is a great diversity of qualities. As we approach, for example, the northern areas of Canada, we find wheat land on which the costs of production are only just covered by the price of the wheat; the land is almost worthless. But the price is an indica-tion that the world demands wheat to such extent that it is willing to pay to have this land cultivated; the land is marginal. Just as the more efficient entrepreneur received a profit when the total demand could only be satisfied by the production of the less efficient ones, so the owners of better land than the marginal will get a rent, determined by the difference between their costs (excluding rent) and those which must be paid on the worst land. The community cannot get the required quantity of the product any cheaper; they must pay enough for the last amount produced to ensure that it will be produced without loss.

Thus we have the general principle that free competition causes price to move towards marginal cost and marginal cost towards price; and when we add as costs the rents and profits, which are the costs to be attributed to superior advantage, the marginal costs are equal to the average costs. Average costs are as low as is compatible with the output, for they will only be reduced if less is demanded than before.[1] The whole productive mechanism is engaged in producing monetary values; the consumer sees that these values are the same to him per unit of money expended [2] and the entrepreneur that the factors of production receive amounts equal to their contribution, or if this cannot be ascertained, what they

[1] It will be seen that we have assumed that all costs are rising ones, with full competitive equilibrium.

[2] This neglects any question of consumer's surplus on the earlier units of each commodity bought. Even if this concept be accepted, the general argument remains the same.

would contribute if used elsewhere.[1]

Everyone gets an amount equal to the value of the contribution made by the factors which he possesses: in fact, everything is compared through its productive power. This proposition is of importance for our later inquiries, since we have reduced the whole complex of economic quantities to one, which is monetary value expressive of purchasing power, or the conduciveness of goods towards the ends of the consumers.

In this position, nothing can be made more plentiful except by producing more of it and thus, since all the productive resources are employed, less of something else. Since the prices set by the community on the last units of each good were equal before (per unit of cost), they must now be different: the scarcer good dearer and the more plentiful one cheaper, the scarce satisfying a more acute want and the more plentiful a less acute one. What has been lost is greater from the consumer's point of view than what has been gained: the position of competitive equilibrium is also that which satisfies the most urgent (monetary) wants of

[1] We have neglected those unusual cases where several factors of less value elsewhere are combined in fixed proportions, *i.e.* cases of indeterminateness, including quasi-rents, on the ground that we are considering long-period equilibrium.

the consumers.[1] For this reason it may be urged that a rational society would always make this disposition of its productive resources; that is to say, it would produce goods in such quantities that the want-satisfying powers of the last unit of each produced should be proportional to the quantity of productive capacity which the production of this last unit involved.

There is the further advantage that if the wants of the community change, or if cheaper methods of production are discovered, it will pay entrepreneurs to make changes in the quantities or methods of production. For if one demand increases, some others must have decreased: one price will rise and show a profit, the others fall and show a loss, and there will follow a shift of production. And if one entrepreneur discovers a more efficient method of production, only those entrepreneurs who adopt it will be able to continue to produce as profitably as before. The system of competition adjusts production to the demands of the consumers, and passes on to them after a time the benefits of improvements.

The length of the working day will be settled by the workers balancing leisure against the additional income they would receive by work-

[1] For a full discussion of this proposition see Barone, "The Ministry of Production in the Collectivist State", Appendix A in *Collectivist Economic Planning*.

ing longer; the last hour's leisure may be treated as a commodity purchased by the income foregone by not working. Saving is also done automatically according to the valuations of the receivers of income. The purpose of saving is either to have a reserve for future contingencies, or in order to increase future income: savings which are invested become capital which will earn an income according to the rate of interest. Each individual will balance the present satisfaction foregone (by not consuming) against that which he hopes to derive from the possession of a reserve or from a permanent income in the future.

It may therefore be asked why any other system of controlling our economic arrangements should be considered, since the competitive one gives such satisfactory results. The first reason is that it is difficult actually to establish such a system, owing to obstacles which prevent competition from being free, and especially which prevent the productive resources from being moved easily from one entrepreneur to another in search of better prices. We shall consider some of the differences between actual systems and the one we have been treating in outline, in the next chapter; it is possible to argue that a controlled system working to a central plan is better than a competitive one which is working badly.

The second reason is that in the system which we have been considering there will be a wide difference between the incomes received by various members of the community, which depends on the productivity of the factors owned. In particular, those who inherit property will have incomes because the property is productive, and these may be very large. The view is widely held that a more satisfactory use would be made of the production of the community if it were shared out more equally. This cannot be proved but it is believed by many people to be true, and this leads to the demand for a Socialist state, the economic problems of which we shall study in the remainder of the book.

Either reason is in itself a valid one for investigating or advocating a controlled economic mechanism. But it is important for purposes of comparison to understand the difference between a competitive system and a real one, both because we should realise that an actual Socialist state might diverge widely from a theoretical one, as an actual competitive one does from a theoretical one: and because the results of a Socialist state should be compared with the actual rather than the theoretical results of competition.

CHAPTER III

DIFFICULTIES IN ACTUAL ECONOMIC SYSTEMS

ALTHOUGH there is a certain amount of freedom of contract in most societies, they do not usually get very near to the state of equilibrium which we have been considering. Freedom of contract is considerably circumscribed by the actions of Governments and of other bodies, and productive resources cannot be moved at all easily, so that the quantities of goods being produced are never adjusted to the changes which are continually taking place. Great complexities are also found because the monetary medium is neither used by the public nor controlled by the authorities in the way in which it was assumed that this would be done at the beginning of the outline of the last chapter.

In the first place, the state supplies various services and pays for them through taxation: this is an arbitrary choice of what the members are to have and in many cases is quite easy to justify, to those who think that individuals should be free to spend their incomes as they please, on the ground that it is agreed by everyone that these services are desirable but that the competitive framework would not supply them so well as does some central body. We have already mentioned public health services as an example. Scarce resources are also required for the supply of such services as defence, justice, and security, which would come high in the order of urgency of most individuals if the state did not arrange for them and if it were possible to make arrangements for their supply to individuals, which would usually be difficult. Many states, or public bodies, also supply goods or services which could be supplied by competition, either because they consider that they can do this more cheaply or reliably than could private entrepreneurs (for example, water supplies by local authorities), or because they wish the supplies to be consumed in some other proportions than would be the result of free purchases (for example, public education). In these cases there is some other criterion than the amount people are prepared to sacrifice to obtain the goods; and it is often difficult to know whether the cost represents the minimum average cost of the service.

States also restrict the field of private enterprise to a marked extent in the pursuit of a variety of ends, and they encourage enterprises which would not be profitable if they had to sell to an open market. They pay subsidies to industries which they consider especially worthy of support, as the beet sugar industry in England; they prevent competitors expanding their production and thus equalising prices and costs, as in the hop-growing and coal industries in England; almost every state prevents various products from entering its boundaries from abroad, in order to reduce the losses or increase the profits of home industries. Through taxation they place heavy burdens on industries, and thus increase their costs and their equilibrium prices and diminish their sales, as in the cases of tobacco and alcoholic drinks in England. They prevent altogether or strictly control the sales of goods which they consider harmful to the consumers, such as narcotic drugs and certain poisons. They make regulations limiting the freedom of contract, such as the laws limiting the hours of work of labourers and the conditions in which work shall take place, and sometimes the rates of pay. The Factory Acts and the Trade Board Acts are examples of this in England. Building Codes and Town Planning Acts restrict the liberty of the individual to build where and how he pleases. Such a catalogue as this could be extended and discussed at length: some examples and the reasons for them will be considered more fully below. The ends served are sometimes those of a majority, sometimes of small groups; it is often the opinion of economists that there is a contradiction about some of these activities, in the sense that more expensive ways are chosen to carry out the plans explicitly stated to be the objective than are necessary with the existing scarcity of resources. This may be due to ignorance, or because some apparently incidental end is that which is really sought by the executive agent.

When we examine the field of private enterprise, it is found that the assumption that entrepreneurs take no notice of the effect that their individual sales have on the prices of their products is often inapplicable. This is the case where some monopolistic position can be obtained, so that the field of entry into some branch of production is restricted. The state assists this process by the granting of patents and copyrights, in order to encourage inventions and discoveries. It is clearly to the interest of each producer to obtain a monopoly if he can, as in this way his profits can be maintained; the existence of the monopoly prevents the entry of competitors and the reduction of

31

price to cost of production. A monopolist will be enabled to experiment with the output and the price, and can make his profits a maximum if he fixes output so that the total sales multiplied by average profit per unit sold will be a maximum. In this case the consumers pay more for the commodity than they would with competitive behaviour, and as fewer resources are used here, more must be used elsewhere: other commodities are somewhat cheaper and we have given reasons for supposing that the consumer's position is not as favourable as it might be. Opinions differ as to the prevalence of monopolistic elements in actual economic systems. It has recently been asserted by a number of writers[1] that most of the retail market has these elements. It is probable that many of them are transitory but that they are always present in a large number of prices, not necessarily the same ones from period to period.

This is particularly the case in the price of many kinds of labour, owing to the formation of associations which try to prevent others from entering the occupations where these exist. The most successful are professional associations and the most obvious, Trade

[1] For example, Professor Chamberlin, Mrs. Robinson, R. F. Harrod.

Unions. These bodies depress the wages of other labourers, or produce unemployment, and enhance their own. In the same way, associations of producers are formed which limit the output of their commodity in order to keep up the price; and sometimes even to destroy some of what has been produced already, a proceeding which in the eyes of the consumers is a negation of economic effort. It is difficult to maintain such associations with success for long periods, but they can affect prices to a marked degree for short ones. In recent years we find that, among other commodities, the sale of wheat, rubber, coffee, sugar, tin, and pepper has been restricted.

All the activities so far considered have been called frictional forces, but it seems better to keep this name for another class of phenomena. This is due to ignorance and to the cost of moving resources already engaged from one kind of production to another. The outline already given of the competitive system indicated a tendency, among those who are attempting to improve their incomes, to choose the most profitable among the alternative fields of production or employment before them. And there is little doubt that most men behave in this way. But owing to the changes which are continually occurring in the independent variables of the system, changes in the desires of consumers, changes in the methods of production, and changes in the resources available, there is always a disparity between the actual dispositions of resources and those dispositions to which individual interests would bring them. The economic system is continually moving towards new positions and is always far from any of those which it is attempting to reach. This is inherent in any system which is changing and it is not necessary to free competition that there should be no frictional forces, though if there were none it might be called perfect competition.[1] But the results which are theoretically possible are much modified in practice because of these forces.

They are easy to understand. It is not surprising that ignorance is present in any sphere, and in the economic world it is to the interest of anyone who has been placed in a favourable position, either fortuitously or as a result of his own efforts, to conceal his good fortune from possible rivals. Much is done both in technical journals and through such state activities as the Department of Scientific and Industrial Research, to spread information about new

---

[1] There is no agreement about terminology in this matter. See Mrs. Robinson, "What is Perfect Competition?" *Quarterly Journal of Economics*, Nov. 1934.

processes, but much must also be concealed. It is extremely difficult to obtain accurate information about the amount of any firm's profits, and even when this is known the exact reason for them remains a matter of conjecture. It is hard for the workers to find out where there are better-paid occupations, to save enough to be trained for them, and to find the money to move to them. The reluctance to leave familiar spots should not be counted as frictional, as it may be a satisfaction worth some monetary sacrifice to remain where one is. It is almost impossible to move capital which has once taken the form of buildings and machines to some new form of production; it might as well be worked until it is worn out or until the value of the product no longer covers the costs which are avoidable if the movable resources are shifted. But every mistake in the investment of capital reduces the output of the productive mechanism to a figure less than would have been attained if it had not been made. We shall give reasons below (p. 87) for thinking that even the rate of interest which corresponds to the scarcity of capital at any moment is never known closely.

Such are some of the ways in which human activities and material obstructions prevent the adjustment of economic systems to the position described as that of competitive equilibrium. But except for the action of Governments, which should perhaps be taken as part of the data, the state of affairs within which the economic problem has to be solved, there is always a tendency towards equilibrium and it is certain that the more acute the disparity, the more rapid will be the adjustment. We spend our incomes carelessly, but we try to avoid the repetition of serious mistakes: the larger the profits or the losses, the more strenuous is the endeavour of entrepreneurs to expand or to contract; the higher the incomes of a particular class rise above current levels, the more entrants will there be to their occupations, as is shown by the tendency, which Adam Smith noticed, to overstock the professions in which there are striking prizes. In every part of the field but one, a departure from equilibrium immediately creates interests which tend to check it. It is this, the monetary problem, which we must now consider.

It will be remembered that we assumed a constant stock of money, continuously spent. All that is really necessary is that it should be spent evenly, since the price system can and does adjust itself to any stock of money, though large changes in quantity are disturbing. But we do not spend all our incomes, holding some of them in the form of ready money or bank balances in order to be able to meet possible emergencies. If for any reason, other than an inflation, the amounts held in this way are increased, the amounts spent will decrease to the same extent, and hence the money offered for goods: prices tend to fall. As they fall, marginal entrepreneurs make losses, and those who cannot finance these will close down and the factors they were employing become unemployed. It takes a long period to reduce wages and it is sometimes difficult to reduce other payments at all, so that the factors of production remain idle.

This reduces output and should thus prevent a further fall in prices. But those parts of incomes which are saved and usually handed over to the entrepreneurs in order to finance the purchase of new capital goods, are unlikely to be spent at all when old-established industries are in a position where they can hardly cover their costs: the value of money in goods is rising, and the value of real capital falling, so that it pays to hold money. Thus the tendency for prices to fall is cumulative once they have begun to go down; money is hoarded (usually by not drawing cheques on bank balances) because no-one is willing to spend it except for current expenditure on

37

goods for immediate consumption, and this hoarding offsets the reduction in output. This is a depression, which is characterised by reductions in incomes, in employment, and, as we should expect, by reductions in the production of new capital goods. As the reduction of incomes proceeds, it becomes more difficult to save and to accumulate money, and the difficulties in which the country finds itself may lead to increased expenditure by the state. There will also be tendencies to reduce the payments to the factors of production, including wages and the rate of interest demanded by any owner of new capital who is prepared to invest it at all. As soon as money is no longer withheld from circulation, the price-level will become steady and the tendencies towards equilibrium, always present, will begin to be felt. But there is at present no agreement among those who have studied this question about the order of causes in passing from a depression and it is probable that any among a number of stimulating agencies may be effective. It is a fact of experience that at some stage the pessimistic feelings of entrepreneurs about the future either change of themselves or are changed by the combination of steady prices and falling costs; for all depressions have been followed by upward movements. It is clear that the forces which allowed the depression to appear—the withholding of money from circulation — provide a pool of money or credit which can be returned and thus can cause an upward movement of prices; and an upward movement will make it profitable to employ money rather than to keep it idle. The anticipation of rising prices brings them about to the extent that holders of money balances are willing to take advantage of the rise, which may continue beyond the point at which prices would remain if people kept their money stocks at the figure they consider appropriate to times of steady prices. But the rise cannot continue indefinitely, for at some point all who had balances which they were willing to deplete must have exhausted them; prices will stop rising, and any attempt to restore depleted balances (for example, by selling goods which have been bought on the rising market) will cause a downward movement, thus initiating a new cycle.

There is an enormous volume of literature on this subject, the practical effect of which has been small; probably because conditions of rigidity in the price structure have been accentuated since the war, rather than because the problem is not understood. It is, in the writer's opinion, self-evident that there could not be changes in the level of prices *and* of the volume of production *in the same direction* for periods as long as four years unless there were changes in the active monetary circulation at the same time; it is the failure of the forces towards equilibrium to produce any effect which constitutes the support of the view that monetary causes are the most efficient of those which are active during the Trade Cycle.[1]

The extreme waste involved in the Trade Cycle has led to a widespread demand for some kind of interference by the State; and Socialism, which we shall now consider, is one of the methods by which its control or alleviation is advocated.

---

[1] See Hayek, *Monetary Theory and the Trade Cycle*, for an account of this paradox. I do not, of course, suggest that Professor Hayek would endorse the very compressed account of Trade Cycle theory just given: my own views owe much to J. M. Keynes.

CHAPTER IV

SOCIALISM

IT is evident that an economic system based on
competition and free contract works through
the decisions of individuals, each of whom is
concerned mainly to improve his own economic
position. The fact that resources seek the most
productive employments with respect to monetary demand is not due to any conscious
activity by the community through political
and other institutions, except to the extent
that a policy of non-interference is deliberately
pursued. And notwithstanding all the activities
of modern states, the main economic structure
of most countries is still similar to that which
we have described.

In a Collectivist or Socialist system, on the
other hand, the economic problem is to be
solved by conscious decision of a social character: the representatives of the community who
dispose of political power decide on the nature
of the price system. This involves the abandon-
ment of free choice to the individual, at any
rate as a fundamental liberty: consumption

and production must fit into a central scheme. Many types of Collectivism are possible, but we shall consider only one of these, Socialism. Some people wish the state to enter the economic field in order to overcome the difficulties which prevent the actual system from working properly, taking the view that competition is so wasteful that central co-ordination is the only solution from which anything can be hoped. This view is behind much of the demand for "planning": the retention of private property and enterprise, within narrower limits than at present indeed, is not incompatible with such plans. But it is the fundamental purpose of Socialism to attain as much economic equality as is compatible with the necessities of production, either on the ground that our ethical judgement commands us directly to do this, or because it is believed that the total of human satisfactions will be greater if incomes are similar than if they show wide divergences. As no-one has yet discovered any method of comparing the states of mind of different people, these views are only opinions and must be taken as given ends of any community which has committed itself to them.

Now men are clearly different from an economic point of view; that is to say, they are capable of producing goods or services which have different exchange values, and so it is impossible to have a system of free exchanges which will not lead to the acquisition of property; and if this can be inherited there will soon be permanent differences of income, whatever the starting-point in this respect. These can be reduced somewhat by heavy taxation, especially by income taxes and death duties; but the experience of Great Britain since the war suggests that no practicable taxation will produce sufficient economic equality to be acceptable to Socialists. It is possible to argue that the policy of weakening the position of capitalist entrepreneurs in the short-period interests of the lower-paid grades of labour has the effect of impairing first the adaptiveness and then the productive capacity of communities based on private property: the economic history of Australia is an example. If the economic position is to be maintained, there is a point after which it becomes necessary to provide an organisation to replace the one we have been considering.

To avoid the accumulation of property, it is necessary that all resources should be disposed of by the state, and in particular that no-one shall be allowed to employ other people for his own profit: all material possessions must be consumption capital, such things as toothbrushes, pictures, and houses. We shall assume that this is to be the fundamental condition of the society which is to be discussed, while a subsidiary condition is that incomes are to be as equal as is practically possible. The first condition is unequivocal, but the second must be considered as lacking definition at the moment. (The reasons for this are, first, that it is probable that the total volume of production and therefore the *average* level of incomes will vary according to how much difference of income is permitted; and second, that it is doubtful whether incomes can be compared without taking account of the kind of work done.)

Various schemes have been put forward by Socialists for the organisation of the state, but the economic arrangements are usually discussed without precision. We shall not consider any type of Communism, in the original sense of indiscriminate sharing.[1] Nor shall we discuss Syndicalism nor Guild Socialism. It is clear that in a collectivist state there are no *necessary* economic relations, and that these might have a completely arbitrary character not susceptible of a deductive analysis. For since some central

---

[1] The modern sense refers to the revolutionary method of achieving Socialism as opposed to the gradual methods of Socialists.

body imposes the forms of economic activity on the community, it *can* impose anything which it has the power to enforce. And a wide diversity of systems becomes possible, depending upon the aims which societies of this kind set before themselves.

Yet if the society acts rationally from an economic point of view, it should be possible to make an analysis of an economic kind. For among the ends chosen there must be some which need to be satisfied or served by the use of scarce resources, and the ordinary problem arises—that of choosing between various uses not all of which are possible at the same time— and there emerges a system of valuations expressive of the economic arrangements. In fact most projected societies of a Socialist character are concerned to a large extent with economic matters and their advocates represent to those whom they attempt to persuade that an economic advantage is obtainable by adopting them. If a Socialist state sets out to do certain things, there is one particular way in which they can be done which is more economic than any of the others, and the expression of this is *the* price system for such a state. If we think that rational behaviour in economic matters is that which gives least scarcity, a rational state will act in the same way as a

45

rational individual. An economic act is defined as that which secures a given end with the least expenditure of scarce resources; it may have all sorts of other aspects but its economic character depends on the relation between the satisfaction obtained and the alternative satisfactions which have to be foregone.

It is sometimes argued that it does not matter whether the price mechanism of a Socialist state is an economical one or not. If this means that mistakes must be tolerated for the sake of the other advantages, the position is perfectly logical and everyone is free to choose between the mistakes of one system (e.g. a capitalist one) and another. But if it means that it is not necessary to have some criterion for the choices which the leaders of the state will have to make, it seems to betray ignorance of the process involved in all choices. Every choice that is made expresses some sort of preferences and the result of all of them is a price system, which is only a set of relative valuations expressed in terms of one of the things which are being compared: this is a necessary simplification if practical results are sought where there is a large number of possible choices. To suppose that prices, rents, rates of interest, because they appear in a capitalist society, should have no place in a Socialist one, is to confuse the essential function of these as a means to a rational choice, with their function as generating incomes to individuals. It is as if it were argued that since wage-earners have to eat in order to be fit to work for employers, therefore in a Socialist state this bourgeois function should be abolished.

A different argument is that which asserts that the benefits to be derived from scarce goods diminish rapidly as their quantity increases, and that all the important wants of individuals can be satisfied without resorting to the intricacies of money and consumer's choice.[1] This will need a fuller discussion. The advantages of this position are the simplicity of the economic mechanism and the difficulty of criticising it; if individual choice is not a guide to individual ends, or if these are of no social importance, the studies of economists become to a large extent of no practical use— like a work on ballistics which assumed the force of gravity to be negative.

We must decide therefore whether a Socialist state is going to act in what economists would

[1] *E.g.* M. Dobb in "The Problems of a Socialist Economy", *Economic Journal*, Dec. 1933: "There is no warrant for assuming that the index which a free market would provide would be preferable to what could be constructed in other ways" (p. 594). The opposite point of view is well stated by A. P. Lerner, *Review of Economic Studies*, Oct. 1934.

47

call a rational way with regard to its resources, and the extent to which it will consult the consumers. If it disposes of sufficient force, it can impose any ideas which it chooses on the community, up to the limit of the productive resources which are available. But even here it must construct an order of preference, since it is inconceivable that all the possibilities which occur to its leaders can be satisfied together. For example, a community which fixes its ideas on military conquest would have to set aside whatever resources were necessary to feed, shelter, and educate its members, leaving only the remainder available for the conduct of its wars. The same limit is set whatever it chooses —our previous examples were the construction of pyramids or the pursuit of higher mathematics—only those resources are free which are not required to satisfy those wants which must be met if the community is to continue at all. We can imagine such a community, with a devotion to some end purely external to the particular welfare (of a material nature) of the individuals which compose it. Military dictatorships and religious communities may approach such a condition. And for them the pricing problem is comparatively simple, since all the resources are really engaged on the production of the same thing, the necessary food, etc., being subsidiary processes towards the common end. But unless there is some grand conception of this sort, the choice between alternatives must be faced.

We can go so far as to say that everyone who is choosing between alternatives, both of which he cannot have with the material at his disposal, is performing an economic act. There must be calculation, whether it is conscious or not. But the results of the calculation are likely to be poor ones if no unit is employed and if the calculator is unaware of what he is doing. The discussion is only obscured if examples are taken of the early wants common to all consumers, the cases where rationing and free choice give the same answers. We know in a vague way what people want at present, and we could make a statistical inquiry which would show us exactly what their wants are— but this would be derived from existing prices. Anyone who thinks that it is easy to tell what is going to be good for the community is either imposing his own ideas or unconsciously using his experience of prices which express the consumers' ideas.

It is quite possible not to consult the consumers at all, or only in a very rough way. For example, it might be decided that everyone should work six hours a day and get so much food, shelter, clothing, and entertainment. The result would be a rationing system, such as is found to a large extent in schools and armies— the consumers take what they are given. Choice is very limited; presumably they get the right sizes of boots and clothing, and there is no reason why the pressure of public opinion should not change any obviously distasteful product—a sort of rudimentary consumer's choice.

As has been said, this has the advantage of simplicity if the state is willing to keep to broad lines of production which it finds by experience to be more or less satisfactory. Pressure may be brought to bear on the community, accustoming it to consume what is available; and there is no doubt that a certain rude plenty could be secured. It is at any rate plausible to argue that many of the actual wants in a competitive society are of a kind which leave the consumer in the same or a worse position after he has endeavoured to satisfy them, if we look any deeper into his psychology than the superficial and indeed circular statement that he only buys what he wants.[1] And we may agree with those who argue in this way that there is need of more investigation than has been made so far into

[1] Cf. Dobb, *loc. cit.*

the connection between wealth and welfare, between what men say that they want and what they really want.[1]

These arguments go behind ordinary economic investigations, which deal with the way men behave rather than with what lies beneath their behaviour. But it must be admitted that most economists suppose that there is some connection between what men say they want and what they do want. If we do not really want to satisfy most of what we assert to be our wants, our behaviour is contradictory and irrational; any authority legislating for the average man must impose on him what it discovers in some independent manner to be good for him. The dangers of such proceedings are only too obvious. Once it is admitted that it is in anyone's interests to impose the ideas of someone else upon him, the possibility of error is very great and the way is open for persecution and intolerance. No body of men can decide on every detail of the individual's requirements when there is a large community to be dealt with, so that standardisation must be followed; and the requirements of the standard individual must be chosen with an end in view

---

[1] There is an elementary discussion of some of the questions involved in *Earning and Spending*, by the author.

which is only approximately that of any actual person.

What is to be gained by such a standardised system of rationing? As we have said, ease and simplicity of operation; to which we may add, in anticipation of a consideration to be discussed later, the advantages of mass production. On the other hand, if we accept the hypothesis that there is some gain in satisfaction from giving people what they want, the losses due to erroneous decisions may well be large. If the economic system aims at the satisfaction of wants, and the purpose of the state is the happiness or welfare of its members, we cannot escape the conclusion that it is necessary to find out what people want before supplying goods. When the resources are scarce it is waste to supply any but the most urgent wants: there is a loss when any want which is satisfied thereby precludes the satisfaction of a more intense one. And there can be little doubt that a rationing system which goes beyond the primary necessities of life will constantly find itself with supplies of goods which are hardly wanted at all.

These considerations would perhaps not move the statesman who had made up his mind that he knew what was for the good of his people better than they. But it has often been pointed out that if goods are distributed in an arbitrary way among individuals, a series of exchanges is bound to arise among them: the man who prefers beer to cider will get rid of his cider for beer to the man who has opposite tastes. A multitude of examples will readily occur to anyone who considers the matter. The waste involved in the barter which would be necessary if the state were not prepared to facilitate these exchanges is as great as in any economic system without money; it comes chiefly from the fact that it is difficult to find someone who has what you want and who wants what you have at the same time. The fact that these exchanges would undoubtedly occur shows us that a rationing system is only one of equality in the sense that everyone gets the same objective parcel of goods; in the sense in which the consumers understand equality it is far removed from it, for it favours the man who is most like the hypothetical average of those who decide on the rations, and the less an individual's tastes are like this, the worse is his position. We can go so far as to say that a state which aims at equality of income *must* give the consumers some choice.

Mr. Aldous Huxley, in his novel *Brave New World*, describes a collectivist state in which the problems of production and distribution from the economic point of view are surmounted by adapting the community to what they are going to get. Instead of adjusting satisfactions to wants, wants are adjusted to the available satisfactions; and this is a method which is possible to all economic systems. It is used in a competitive society to a large extent in a negative way, by the creation of a want which was not felt before in order to increase the sales of some producer's goods and thus to increase his profits; it would have a positive effect either if it informed the consumer of how he could better satisfy a want he feels already, or if it persuaded him that he did *not* want something he thought he did. This is a method of diminishing scarcity which has not yet been properly investigated, but calls our attention to the possibility of simplifying the economic problem somewhat without loss. We shall see later that changes always have a disturbing effect, and that some loss of variety might be justified if, as a result, losses of a frictional nature could be avoided. But at present we do not know whether we should like our tastes to be imposed on us in this way; and if our wants are satisfied in any other way without consulting us, the arguments above appear to be valid against any form of rationing in general, and therefore in favour of retaining the choice of consumers.

Let us now consider in more detail the question of the kind of goods to be supplied. We may begin with those which are clearly indicated as necessary but which are clearly unsuited to free choice. Like a capitalist society, the Socialist one must have Government services: the police, the defence forces, the administration of justice and of the laws generally (including the important department which is to be responsible for directing the work of production). These present no difficulty, because they are wanted by the community but are not consumed by any individuals as such—the state is the proper authority to exercise choice, taking the opinions of anyone who can be consulted with the given political mechanism. The administrative departments are almost a technical problem, in which the ends to be reached are given as unities and the means for reaching them efficiently must be found. What is wanted is an equitable administration of justice, and the economic question of how much is unimportant. We should not go too far in this direction; such police activities as traffic control clearly involve decisions as to how much is justified, but if any decisions at all are technical they are to be found here.

55

The next class of wants is more difficult—those in which the consumer could exercise a choice, but would not consume as much as might be thought desirable on other grounds. The best examples are provided by education and public health. Owing to their lack of experience, children rarely take precautions in certain directions, but experience shows us that when they grow up they usually agree that it was wise to force these precautions upon them. Nor can parents be trusted to make satisfactory choices on behalf of their children; even when they act generously they may be affected by sentiment, prejudice, or ignorance. And similarly with regard to preventive medicine, drains and sewers, vaccination and precautions against contagious diseases; the individual cannot be left to himself if his neighbours are to achieve satisfactory results, nor does he really wish to be. It is not intolerant to act on the assumption that no-one wishes for smallpox or typhoid fever, whatever he may say: an authoritative system is far the best. The individual will not do when he is active what he agrees to be desirable when he is reflective. Everyone will agree that there ought to be a universal system of public health, and few would stand out against universal public education. But because the immediate effects of neglect are usually small, it is probable that many will not do for themselves as much as they feel that their neighbours should do. They must be forced to have as much as they want: there is no danger of wasteful consumption as there would be if there were a free supply of goods more immediately pleasant.

The difficulties begin when such questions as those concerning the kind and size of defence forces and the quality and quantity of education are considered. There must be a legal and police system, and the laws governing social relationships can be enacted without much reference to economic considerations; there must be a public health department. The size of all three depends primarily on the efficient performance of the services considered necessary. Military experts may perhaps decide on the kind of army wanted: it is doubtful whether educational experts should be left to decide on the kind of education. But neither are in a position to say how large their organisations are to be; the larger they are the less will be available for other wants. Every soldier is a potential plough-boy, mechanic, or entertainer whose services will be lost when he performs military duties. Calculation is inevitable.

But whether in a Socialist or any other state, the Government is the only body which can make these calculations. There has to be an arbitrary element in them, the uncertainty of the deciding agency as to the weight to be attached to the results of a unit of expenditure in one direction rather than another. In an ordinary capitalist state, the Chancellor of the Exchequer is supposed to try to make every use of the money extracted from the taxpayer of equal marginal usefulness or utility, and each equal to the use that the taxpayer would have made of the money if it had been left with him. As there are no tests by which these matters may be decided, he has to go by his practical judgement and that of the Cabinet. In the same way, the directing body of a Socialist state has to decide how much defence is required, having regard to the position of foreign affairs and the general level of production; how much education can be afforded: and so on. There is no way of reaching decisions except through guess-work and common sense. They must be made, and only the Government can make them.

Some line must now be drawn between the goods which are to be supplied in this way and those in the supply of which the consumer is to be consulted directly. In all cases where a line has to be drawn, it is found that there is a region of uncertainty. The existence of this should be taken as an indication that it does not matter exactly where the line is drawn, as it is probably indifferent for practical purposes where it comes. The only requirement is to be certain that it is not demonstrably in the wrong place. In this case, it is apparent that it would be ridiculous to consult the individual in matters of public health or defence; it is equally ridiculous to decide arbitrarily on what he should eat or the colours he should wear. For it can be of little importance to the ordinary man what his neighbour eats or wears, while it is of great importance to him what he does himself in this way. We shall assume from now on that there is a field of some importance, that of ordinary consumable commodities, in which it will be decided to find out what the consumers want before supplying them with goods.

This could be done by means of questioning or voting, but the results would be inaccurate and the difficulties immense. Since there will not be enough to supply everybody's wants, an order of preference will be required. But until an individual knows how much he is going to have of a commodity he cannot say how much he wants it, while his decision will in any case be affected by what he is going to get of other things. He will be very much in the dark until he knows what is going to be available and in what proportions. In short, any system of direct inquiry will be cumbrous, imperfect, and necessitating constant changes; and, as we have said in connection with rationing, it will lead to the setting up of a series of barter transactions.

It is thus inevitable that there should be prices and a mechanism which uses them. There can be economic arrangements without prices as such; but they are made in the dark, with guesses at exactly those quantities which are known accurately through a price system. As Pareto says:[1] "Les prix . . . peuvent disparaître . . . comme entités réelles, mais ils demeureront comme entités comptables; sans eux le *ministère de la production* marcherait à l'aveugle et ne saurait comment organiser la production". The task of allocating productive resources to different uses is almost impossible without some form of pricing; the wrong things will be made in the wrong quantities, and the directors of the productive processes will be unable to find out what, if anything, is amiss. These statements will become clearer as the task to be performed is realised.

[1] *Manuel*, p. 362.

A price system implies that the consumers shall have incomes representing what portion of the available stock of goods it is thought each should have; and that they should choose among these goods, each of which has a fixed price, to the extent of their purchasing power: thus they indicate their preferences automatically. Everyone gets what he wants: if he likes what is dear he must pay for it, and in this sense he is worse treated than someone who likes what is cheap. But each man can put himself in the position of anyone else when he comes to repeat his purchases, for he can buy what anyone else with the same amount of money is buying. By selecting that price system which will just get rid of the available goods, the best use will be made of them, in the sense that each consumer will satisfy his most urgent wants. The difficulty inherent in rationing, that some like one thing and some another, is avoided, for each chooses what he wants most. This has already been discussed in connection with the analysis of the competitive society. It will be remembered that an increase of price almost always reduces the amount of a good which will be bought, since the dearer it is the more of other goods must be foregone in order to obtain it; and similarly, a reduction of price makes it more attractive in comparison with other things and increases the amount bought. A price can always be found which will just clear the available stock of any good, leaving no-one who was willing to pay that price unsatisfied.

CHAPTER V

THE AIM OF THE ECONOMIC SYSTEM

WE shall assume in future that, unless explicitly stated, there is no private property in the means of production; that there are a number of wants which it has been decided to satisfy through a price system and the choice of consumers; and that the economic system has already reached a fairly advanced stage of industrialisation, and comprises a population of at least some millions. The reasons for the latter provisos may be stated here in anticipation of later conclusions. It appears to the writer that a small community is unsuitable for accurate economic calculations, which require comparisons between a number of undertakings which produce the same kind of goods; while it is doubtful whether they can be made at all in a backward one. For it would be difficult to get information and to make the decisions of the central authority mean anything even if the information could be collected. This does not mean that small or backward communities cannot have a Socialist organisa-

63

tion: in some ways central control is easier to enforce when one man finds it possible to grasp all the important data and to survey the whole field in which his decisions are being executed. But the success of Robinson Crusoe or of the family farm, or of the small Socialist community, depends on the character and ability of the controlling individual; no apparatus of calculation is required, for perception and action are combined. In a complex economic unit such as we are envisaging, it is quite impossible for any individual to make all the decisions from a mere inspection of the daily life of the people: a theoretical study of the problem is essential. In this chapter it is proposed to give some theoretical consideration to the problems which will confront those responsible for the organisation of a Socialist economic system, when the conditions assumed are present. Following Barone, the responsible authorities may be referred to as the Ministry of Production.

It has sometimes been suggested that they should produce the maximum of happiness (ophelimity) for the community. This involves the assessment of the capacity of each individual for enjoyment or self-expression, an impossible task: in the present state of human knowledge, we cannot compare the states of mind of two individuals, and this must be done before a beginning could be made with the problem of maximum ophelimity. Even the pattern of income distribution cannot be considered without reference to the necessities of production, and its consideration will be deferred. The Ministry of Production must see that there is some form of money and that the consumers have known money incomes, the amounts of which are not important for the present. It is necessary also that there should be available to the Ministry an estimate of the size of the public services, either in the form of an absolute quantity (*e.g.* 800 policemen, or 40 gallons of water per head per day), or as a proportion of the available resources (*e.g.* 10 per cent of the national income on education). Such estimates will, of course, be tentative, but as has been explained in the last chapter these decisions must be made in some more or less arbitrary way.

The first problem is to dispose of the goods which are produced so that they satisfy the most intense wants of the consumers, as indicated by their own preferences expressed through the manner in which they dispose of their incomes. The publicly provided goods or services must be assumed to be high in the list of preference of the community as a whole,

65

i.e. to be goods which would have been chosen to the extent to which they are actually available, if the consumers had been free to take them or other alternatives in any proportions they pleased. Or, if it is preferred, we can say that these goods have to be consumed and produced, and that it is only with the remainder that endeavours will be made to adjust allocation to consumers' preferences.

This problem presents no theoretical difficulty: it is usually admitted by critics of Socialist economics in general that this is so. The condition is satisfied when the goods are sold at prices which just clear the market, as has been explained in Chapters II and IV: the mechanism required will be considered below.

The second problem is to produce the goods in such proportions that the prices which clear the market of them also represent their cost to the community as expressed in other goods which might have been made instead. It has been explained in Chapter II that it is only when this condition is satisfied that the resources are producing as much as possible. For if given resources are actually producing one thing and are capable of producing another, and if the consumers prefer the second to the first, then it is to their advantage that the production of the second should be increased and of the first diminished until from the changes in scarcity they are indifferent between them.

This problem presents such difficulties that many writers assert that it is impossible of solution, and hence that no Socialist state is possible in which rational economic calculation can be made. In a capitalist society the operation of competition tends continually to bring price towards cost of production; and the existence of a market for the factors of production ensures that the price of each shall tend towards its value, which is derived from the value which the consumers set upon what it produces. The factors tend to receive the value of their marginal products, and where the same production can be secured by substituting a cheaper for a dearer factor, the substitution will be carried out by the alert entrepreneur. There is thus a constant process of comparing the productive capacities of resources and adjusting their prices to this; and when factor prices measure productivity, and goods are sold at cost, our second condition is satisfied. To the extent that competition is imperfect or absent, this condition will be departed from; but in the opinion of the writer the tendency to correct divergences is always present and the greater they are the more likely will it be that this tendency will become operative.

The difficulty, then, is essentially that of calculating the marginal products of factors of production in alternative uses. It seems desirable to consider at this point the criticisms of those who assert that this cannot be done. A convenient summary of them is given in a book recently published: *Collectivist Economic Planning*.[1] The simplest argument is that raised by Professor Mises, who points out that the valuations of the market are necessary to fix prices, and that it is contrary to the very idea of Socialism that there should be a market for the means of production. Hence "because no production-good will ever become the object of exchange, it will be impossible to determine its monetary value".[2] It follows that even if we can find prices for the finished goods, there will be no costs with which to compare them. The rest of Professor Mises' argument is a deduction from this assertion, and stands or falls with its truth or falsity. He repeats later, "Where there is no free market, there is no pricing mechanism; without a pricing mechanism, there is no economic calculation".[3] The

---

[1] *Collectivist Economic Planning*, edited by F. A. von Hayek.

[2] *Op. cit.* p. 92.   [3] *Op. cit.* p. 111.

latter part of his article is more against the
efficiency than the theoretical possibility of a
Socialist economy.

To Professor Halm the difficulty is the same
but the reasoning not so syllogistic as Professor Mises' "Socialism = no market in means
of production: no market, no prices: therefore
Socialism = no prices for the means of production". Professor Halm refers to the lack of
"the characteristic under-bidding and out-
bidding that is essential for the rapid determination of prices". He must mean the correct
prices, since a central Ministry could determine the actual prices it chose to debit to its
productive organisations with any speed it
pleased. But the thought is clear: that the
apparatus which would have to be used to
determine costs would be cumbersome and unable to work out its results until after the time
when it was required to know them. This is at
any rate more hopeful than the bald assertion
that there is no way of discovering them at all;
since all actual economic systems depart to a
considerable extent from the theoretical position of equilibrium, for reasons suggested in
Chapter III, the advocates of Socialism can
assert that their system would be no more
imperfect than the present ones. It will be
argued later that the Socialist economy can

always clear its markets both of goods and of resources, owing to its control of the monetary system and to the fact that in the short period it can be indifferent to losses and therefore need not close sub-marginal enterprises until alternative occupation is available for the displaced resources. And this is the first essential of a price system.

The difficulty remains, however, of ascertaining the correct factor prices. Professor Halm is most troubled by the rate of interest: *"Now it is unfortunate that this allowance for interest, the need for which is urgently dictated by economic considerations, cannot be adopted in the socialistic economy. Perhaps this is the most serious objection that can be maintained against socialism"*.[1] This argument begins, as does that of Professor Mises, from the absence of bargaining in the capital market. To determine prices, demand and supply must meet in a market, "but there can be no demand and no supply when the capital from the outset is in the possession of its user". If the Ministry of Production controls all the resources, it has no competitors with whom to make comparisons.

Carrying his inquiry further, he considers to some extent the possibility of breaking the circle by deducing the prices of the factors

---

[1] *Op. cit.* p. 161. Italics in text.

from the prices of the consumption goods (for which, of course, there will be a market where the buyers, though not the sellers, compete). But in his opinion it is invalid to deduce the price of the factors from the prices of the goods they produce, unless there is only one single factor of production, *e.g.* homogeneous labour. "For, of course, the essential thing is the possibility of establishing a comparison between *known* commodity prices and *known* costs of production. Any sort of economic calculation that aims at deducing the value of the factors of production from the prices of the commodities is consequently impracticable."[1]

It must be admitted at once that if the prices of the factors can neither be obtained by competitive bargaining nor deduced from the prices of the finished consumption goods, then there seems to be no way of finding them out. But it may be asked how the competitive economy *knows* the prices of the factors: Professors Mises and Halm will reply that it is the result of the meeting of supply and demand in the market. Now it is difficult to see what is behind the demand for the factors of production except the desire of the entrepreneurs to sell the products to the consumers at a profit. Unlike the demand for goods by the consumer,

[1] *Op. cit.* p. 163.

which must be taken as given, it is a derived demand: the known costs of production are known through the interplay of forces one of which is the prices of commodities. Part of the difficulty comes from the treatment of two interconnected quantities as independent.

In the following section [1] Professor Halm considers another aspect of the same question, the difficulty which the Socialist state will find in estimating the value of capital goods already in existence; and asserts that it is not possible to determine the costs of production of capital goods, "for they themselves are the product of labour and capital, and a value must therefore be ascribed to capital in advance in order to permit the determination of the cost of using capital".[2] He sees no way of breaking this circle; nor would it be possible, either in a Socialist state or in any other, if it were impossible to derive factor prices from the prices of products, and to compare factors used in one kind of production with those used in another. Finally, he expresses himself as "extremely dubious" about the possibility of estimating other costs, rents, and wages. It is clear from these quotations that Professor Halm has got beyond Professor Mises' simple proof: but that he considers what is technically

[1] § 13.　　　　　　　[2] *Op. cit.* p. 164.

called the "problem of imputation"—or that
of allocating marginal productivities—to be
insoluble without the competition of entrepreneurs.

Professor von Hayek takes the argument a
stage further and begins by examining the in-
accuracy of cost determination in a competitive economy. The principal difficulty is that
of estimating the proper depreciation allowance to be added to the price when the productive process involves the use of existing capital—when there is a quasi-rent element in the
price. If the process is inaccurate when there is
a market, how much more difficult will it be in
its absence. On the whole, Professor von Hayek
thinks that the difficulties will be more practical than theoretical; and he summarises the
virtues of the competitive system as follows:
"The essential thing about the present economic system is that it does react to some
extent to all those small changes and differences which would have to be deliberately dis-
regarded under the system we are discussing
if the calculations were to be manageable".[1]
He is referring to the suggestion that Socialist
calculation might be made along the line of
the mathematical solution of the equations of
equilibrium, but the criticism is one which

[1] *Op. cit.* p. 212.

would need to be taken seriously against any proposals.

There are two threads to be discovered among the writers we have been discussing. The first is the view that the Ministry of Production will be unable to find a method which is theoretically sound of assessing the costs of production; it will therefore be unable to decide on the prices which it ought to aim at, and its quantitative estimates of the proportions in which it is desirable to produce the different consumption goods will be only guesses and almost certainly wrong. The second view is that it will be so difficult in practice to devise a mechanism which will enforce the results of theoretical calculation that the errors actually made will be of a serious nature. It will be the purpose of the remainder of this chapter to argue that there is no theoretical difficulty in the way of calculating costs, whatever the form of control over production, as long as there is a market in consumer's goods. The practical difficulties are unknown, in the sense that no serious attempt has yet been made to make economic calculations in a Socialist economy. It is possible to indicate some of those which experience suggests will arise; it is the opinion of the writer that the most serious will occur in connection with the rate of interest, as Professors Halm and Hayek suggest.

The value of a unit of a factor of production may be considered in two ways—its actual value and its potential value; and it is the task of the mechanism by which economic adjustments are carried out to bring these two values together. The actual value which the community is deriving from a unit is its specific contribution to the amount of production, at the value which is set upon it by the community, either publicly as in the case of Government services, or as a result of choice in a market. The only theoretical difficulty involved is that of calculating this amount, which must be a quantity between the value of production which will be lost if the unit were removed and the remaining factors rearranged in the most profitable way, and the value of production which will be gained if an additional similar unit were added and the whole process again rearranged as efficiently as possible. For example, the value of the helmsman to the carrying process performed by a ship is not to be calculated by removing him and carrying on with no-one at the wheel; but by removing him and putting another seaman in his place, and so on until the tasks undone because the vessel is short-handed are those of least importance.

75

There is a good deal of literature on this subject and it can hardly be called a controversial one. It is not necessary, as has sometimes been suggested, to know the price of the other factors before we can calculate the value of the one in question; the other factors remain the same throughout, and their price is immaterial. All that is required is the value of the product. The difficulty in computing the marginal product arises from the fact that in practice a whole labourer or machine has to be added or removed, instead of the small fraction which is supposed in the mathematical theory of the subject. Thus it is possible to have a gap between the marginal loss and the marginal gain, and there is an element of indeterminateness in the value of the marginal product. The process of rearrangement is called variation of the technical coefficients,[1] and in some industries this variation is not possible without large changes in output. To take our previous example, if a boat has only one man aboard and he is removed, the loss will be all the value of whatever the boat is doing, while if another man is added there will probably be little change in the value of the combination.

[1] The technical coefficients are the quantities of each factor required to produce a unit of product, *i.e.* the proportions in which the factors are combined.

But it cannot be seriously contended that the difference is important in most cases of labour or with new capital, and since all capital wears out in the course of time, there are constant opportunities of making estimates of the kind required. (We shall see below that the principal difficulty in the case of new capital is connected with the rate of depreciation.) If the business man does not attempt to make such estimates, it is hard to see how he arrives at the proportions in which he combines his productive factors: in fact, he does so, as any conversation with such a man will show—he always replies when asked why he engages a man or buys a machine that he thinks that it will pay. The difficulty in estimating specific productivity is almost entirely found when there are aggregations of capital already in existence. And we shall see that these aggregations, because they are specialised, always derive their value from the value of their outputs; the problem of costing does not arise except when the resources to be costed are transferable.

The problem of assessing marginal productivities, therefore, is mainly practical; it depends on whether the Socialist state can command the services of men as capable as the managers of capitalist factories, and no general answer can be given to the question as to whether this can be done or not. The next problem, however, is much more difficult. The values so far ascertained are not really costs at all, being only deductions from the market values of the goods. What is now required is to form an estimate of the potentialities of the factors in other directions. The costs of the resources to the community are measured by what they could have produced elsewhere;[1] for this measures the loss to the community from employing any resource at any particular operation. And if two units of a factor of production are producing different actual values there will be a gain from a transfer.

So far, we have been speaking of factors of production in the abstract, a habit of economists which conceals the difficulties of the subject. We can now see what is meant when it is asserted that the process of adjustment is only possible when there is a single factor of production: when this is so, there are no difficulties of comparison. But the Ministry of Production has before it perhaps millions of workers, with a wide variety of technical train-

---

[1] It will be seen that no attempt has been made to consider real costs in Marshall's sense of efforts and sacrifices; for the same reason for which we made no attempt to consider maximum "ophelimity".

ing and with abilities ranging from the genius to the mentally deficient—the blanket term "labour" means little more than that they are all human. In the same way, the natural resources, conveniently described as "land", consist of land suitable for a diversity of crops, and with a range of fertility from the best to perhaps barren desert, mines of all kinds, forests, fisheries, waterways. Even the appliances already made and referred to as "capital", although they were probably all in the common form of money at the moment when they were passing from the saving classes or entrepreneurs to the constructors of capital goods, are now specialised in the form of buildings, machines, railway tracks, tools, and so on; and even these classes conceal beneath their names a bewildering medley of objects, each with a specific use.

When it is realised that all these members of the class "factors of production" have to be compared with one another—and this not with respect to their power of satisfying the consumer, nor even with respect to their power of producing in their present uses goods which satisfy him, but with respect to their power of producing *all* the goods which satisfy him— the formidable nature of the next step will be realised. It must be admitted at once that no

79

accurate answer is possible: the demands of consumers, and hence the potentialities of productive resources, change rapidly in comparison with the time which would be required to make a fraction of the comparisons, and the labourers die, the capital goods wear out, before they can be tried in more than a few occupations.

It is not to be supposed that any society, even in those short periods of history when free competition was thought by the ruling classes to be the ideal of an enlightened government, approached the point when all resources are applied in accordance with the principles which have been laid down. We have considered in Chapter III some of the frictional and institutional difficulties in the capitalist state; and it appears that legal obstructions and monopolistic activities create new disequilibria at least as fast as old ones are removed. It is commonly stated by the advocates of a Socialist economy that it will begin with important advantages in this respect; and in particular that there will be equal opportunities for all (and hence a better distribution of labour), and that monopolies will be attempting to equate price and marginal cost instead of marginal revenue and marginal cost. Against this it is clear that unless the Socialist state knows what its costs are, its good intentions with respect to the distribution of resources will be frustrated by its ignorance as to what it ought to be doing.

Recalling Professor Hayek's remark, "The essential thing about the present system is that it does react to some extent", let us consider exactly how this reaction occurs. The moving force is that of self-interest. As Adam Smith put it: "Every man, as long as he does not violate the laws of justice, is left perfectly free to pursue his own interest his own way, and to bring both his industry and capital into competition with those of any other man".[1] The entrepreneurs are constantly trying to substitute cheaper for more expensive resources; and the owners of the factors of production to find those occupations which are most profitable to them. From both sides the work of comparison proceeds constantly; and, the great virtue of the capitalist system, the wider the discrepancy between the actual position and that of the theoretical equilibrium, the more likely is it that there will be a move in the right direction. A monopolist who is content with a profit somewhat larger than the run of competitive profits may lead a quiet life; but if he advertises himself by exploiting his situa-

[1] *Wealth of Nations*, end of Book IV.

tion to the full, he is likely to find that he has attracted so many competitors, against whom he thought himself safe, that the whole industry is ruined by over-production and losses. A Trade Union may hold the level of wages somewhat above that prevailing for similarly skilled work, but let it push its advantage too far and it will find its position undermined in a variety of ways.

In order to form an opinion as to whether the Socialist state can discern serious maladjustments, let us consider each of the ordinary classes of factors of production separately. If we choose any one of them arbitrarily as a unit, what is required is to compare all the others with it: to express each of them in terms of productive capacity—productive, that is, of monetary values.

LABOUR.—In the Socialist state the cost of labour to be used in calculations is not necessarily, nor even probably, the same as the wage; though, as we shall see later, it is probable that incomes will be paid in the form of wages, these will not be the marginal products of the class of labour to which each worker belongs, which we are now endeavouring to find. Let us attempt to rate all the workers in terms of one of them; say the unskilled labourers.

The problem is to divide the labour into groups, the members of which have more or less similar capacities; but with the members of each group non-substitutable for the members of the others. (From a theoretical point of view we may neglect the *specific* training of each man, since this may be altered in a comparatively short period—at most seven years, except for that labour which we shall consider under the head of management.) We are concerned only with inherent differences of ability. It is also necessary to rate the members of each group with respect to all the others by finding a margin at which they may be compared by substitution for one another: an apparent contradiction, since the mark of the groups is to be that they are in general non-substitutable.

Labour is differentiated according to innate capacity and to training. If we have decided on a unit of measurement, in this case the money with which the consumers buy the goods, we can calculate the cost of training: we then require to know the rate of interest and the probable working life of the trained man in order to know how much to charge for his services compared with the untrained. The problem is much the same as that of calculating depreciation and depends for its solution only

83

on whether the rate of interest can be found.[1]
It will be found, however, that some individuals cannot be trained to perform some tasks owing to their lack of ability, and it is almost certain that there will be occupations in which the scarcity of skilled workers will necessitate the restriction of the supply of their products by charging for the workers at a higher rate than the unskilled rate plus cost of training.

The following technique is proposed for dealing with this question and with similar problems which arise in the pricing of other factors of production.

[1] Let a be the cost of the unskilled worker and b be his wage.

Let x be the cost of the skilled worker.

Period of training, n years: cost of this, c per year.

Length of working life, t years.

Rate of interest, r per cent per annum.

There are two possible calculations:

(1) Neglecting the difference between his wage and his output.

Training costs are c per year.

Capital cost of skilled worker is

$$c + c(1+r) + c(1+r)^2 + \ldots + c(1+r)^{n-1} = A \text{ (say)}.$$

This has to be recovered in a period of $t - n$ years.

Annual cost of this $= Ar +$ a sum, B, to recover capital, such that $B + B(1+r) + \ldots + B(1+r)^{t-n-1} = A.$ Hence

$$x = a + Ar + B.$$

(2) If we include the difference between wage and output and consider the marginal utility of money the same for everyone, then instead of c in the above calculation, we must substitute C, where

$$C = c + a - b.$$

If we begin with the price of the skilled labour assumed to be that of unskilled labour plus cost of training (and assume that we know the other costs), then if the demand for the products of the skilled labour is such that the price which clears the market is above the assumed cost, it will be necessary to expand the output. To do this it will be necessary to train fresh labour: in the meantime any expansion of production will be with unskilled labour and at rising costs, so that equilibrium will be reached when the marginal costs equal the price which clears the market. The skilled labour will then be rated at its value derived from the value of the output, and there will be a divergence between the cost of training and this sum. As unskilled labour is trained, production expands, and the value of the output and therefore of the skilled labour falls. But if there is a scarcity of the necessary ability, the marginal costs will still rise with new entrants, and as soon as this happens the expansion should be stopped, with marginal costs equal to prices and with the skilled labour permanently rated at the value of its marginal output, *i.e.* the value of the output of one of the truly skilled men if he were added at the point at which the newly trained ones were applied.

This result should be the same as that which

THE ECONOMIC SYSTEM IN A SOCIALIST STATE

would be obtained by comparing unskilled labour directly with skilled in the particular industry, and indeed the comparison has been made at the time when the industry was attempting to expand with labour of unsuitable quality. The classification into non-substitutable groups can therefore only be understood as a quantitative separation. An unskilled labourer can be trained to be some sort of a carpenter or fitter, but the man who is naturally fitted for the latter occupations will do more carpentering or fitting in the same time.

We must not be misled by the terms of the foregoing argument, and suppose that all the labour will be classifiable into tidy groups with a marked quantitative difference in output between them. Obviously, when we take a large number of men there will be a smooth gradation between the best and the worst, except conceivably in certain tasks of great importance which most men will be unable to do at all. The ideal costing system would be one in which all resources were compared and each costed according to its specific capacities. But this is impossible for practical reasons in any economic system; it would be so cumbersome that its cost would far outweigh the losses which arise from the rough grouping of resources into classes and the estimation of the average productive capacity of the members of each class. All that is really required is some sort of ascending scale of groups, with the scarcity relative to the demand for the services of each group greater in each succeeding case; and a cost figure placed on each by an endeavour to estimate both the rising costs which occur when each group is recruited from the members of the one below it, and the price terms on which the lower group is substituted for the one next above it. The technique of industrial psychologists is already sufficient to give us some idea of the capacities of those who form the material from which the labour forces are to be constituted.

CAPITAL.—This is the most difficult problem which has to be faced. It is necessary to establish both the cost of production of the capital and its marginal productivity in terms of the common unit of value.

THE RATE OF INTEREST.—The accurate determination of the rate of interest involves some theoretical difficulties. In the capitalist system it is impossible in practice to distinguish money from capital: savings are made with money and capital goods bought with it. The rate of interest is supposed to ensure that the use of scarce capital is restricted to those places where it will be most demanded, but in practice it is mainly an indicator of the phase of the trade cycle and depends to a large extent on banking and Government policy. The theory of interest is fairly straightforward if we neglect monetary influences; but no economist has yet produced a theory which takes these influences into account, and which is generally accepted.[1] If by the rate of interest we mean the marginal product of the existing body of capital, it is safe to say that no-one knows what the long-term rate of interest is.

The Socialist state controls the monetary system, and it can be indifferent to changes in the general price-level; it should be able to avoid the difficulties which arise from monetary causes. But it will be necessary that it should form a correct opinion about the amount of its working capital; for otherwise it will be able to support for some time a rate of interest lower than the correct one, by making funds available through monetary expansion, thus causing an unintended diversion of goods from the consumers, and *vice versa*.

Let us assume that when the Socialist Government begins operations there is an existing stock of capital equipment and that it

---

[1] The complexities of the subject are illustrated in *The General Theory of Employment, Interest and Money*, by J. M. Keynes.

is decided to use this. (It will be argued below that its first task will be to accumulate sufficient stocks of material in process to enable it to utilise this equipment.) The effect of this decision is to determine the technical co-efficients, or the period of production if this terminology is preferred, compelling the appropriate saving. It is probable that later, when the rate of interest is discovered, these technical coefficients will be found to be wrong; but this cannot be discovered until a beginning has been made, and all economic systems work by methods of trial and error. The problems of rent and of management will be considered separately, though of course in practice they will all have to be faced at the same time.

The theoretical difficulty from the point of view of the Socialist state is that all capital is essentially similar, since it all represents the results of past production: hence, ultimately it must all be costed at the same rate. But it is impossible to take a particular plant and attempt to calculate the rate of interest directly from the productivity of capital there, since it is hard to know whether the plant is a marginal one and whether the industry of which it forms a part is in equilibrium. Further, a small error in the assumed rate of depreciation will seriously affect the result. Hence the only way that can be adopted is to attempt to choose a rate of interest which will use all the capital but which will not cause a general tendency to expand. As it cannot be calculated directly from the prices of the consumers' goods, which are the only known prices at present, it must be guessed in the first place; and it seems that this is best done from the previous history of the country, taking some point between the extremes reached in the ups and downs of the trade cycle. This should be the long-term rate, and not the more sensitive rate for short money. There seems no reason why there should be a complex of rates in a Socialist society, where there is no particular virtue in liquidity.

Can we now place a price on the working capital or intermediate goods? They will themselves have been produced by labour and capital, and unless they happen to be consumers' as well as producers' goods, so that they have a market price, the same problem re-occurs. Hence it will be necessary to guess the cost of these goods, adding some arbitrary amount to the labour cost, which will be given from the rough classification of labour already made.

We now have estimates for the costs both of labour and of working capital, and can find by subtraction from the value of the output the gross earnings of the fixed capital. A further guess must be made at the annual depreciation of the plant, and we have finally the net earnings, which are the quasi-rent of the plant. Capitalising these at the assumed rate of interest, we have an estimate of the value of the fixed capital, erroneous to an unknown extent owing to the various guesses which have been made.

In arriving at the rate of depreciation, an estimate has been made of the *cost* of replacing the fixed capital, and this must now be checked by reference to the industries which produce capital goods. Their labour will be rated by comparison with similar labour engaged elsewhere, and they should be able to estimate the cost of their own capital: as they know the rate of interest, they can set prices on their products which will cover their costs. There will now be disparities between the costs so reckoned and the values of the plants as deduced from their earning capacities, and it begins to be possible to check the guesses which have been made. Several procedures may be followed according to the intentions of the Ministry with regard to saving: one case will be sufficient for purposes of illustration, that in which it is decided to keep the total amount of capital (estimated by its cost rather than its value) constant.

Existing plants can be classified into three divisions: those whose value is more than their cost (earning a surplus over the assumed rate of interest); those which are earning less than this but covering their expenses for labour and working capital; those which are not covering these expenses, and making a book-keeping loss. The first group should be expanded, the second contracted as the plant wears out, the third contracted as soon as alternative occupations can be found for the labour. And clearly a beginning should be made with those which show the widest disparities between values and costs, since here resources are being of least use (where losses are being made) or greatest (where the difference is positive).

If the rate of interest has been chosen correctly, the total expansions should balance the total contractions. Thus we get our first check on the rate: for if there is a general tendency to expand, the rate must be raised in order to turn some of the apparent profits into losses, and *vice versa*. Changes in the rate will affect all the calculations, and each successive series will be more accurate than the preceding ones: thus we have an indicator by which to control the original guesses.

Since the capital is specialised, the expansion and contraction will be a slow business. In order to keep the capital intact, the size of the capital good industries must be just enough to make good depreciation; but in the early stages, when they are not replacing those industries which are too large, there will be surplus capacity with which to enlarge the plants or industries which are to be expanded. The capital-good industries have to work to order, always selling their products at cost (or rather transferring them in accordance with the Ministry's order of priority); their size has been fixed, and though their form must be adapted according to the character of the industries which they have to keep efficient, they will not work according to apparent profits or losses as do all the other industries. When the capital has finally taken the required shape, expansions or contractions will occur only under the stimulus of changes in the tastes of the consumers.

So far we have provided a rough guide to the rate of interest: as the process gets into working order and there is some confidence in the figure and in the costs of the working capital, a second process can be begun. This is the making of experiments of variation in individual plants: directly ascertaining the productivity of the capital employed by computing the change in output which would occur with a changed amount of capital. The figures thus obtained will vary from plant to plant and contain errors due to mistakes in the allowance for depreciation; it would be hopeless to attempt to check the rate of interest directly from them. But by comparing these figures with the assumed rate of interest, it can be seen whether larger amounts of capital in relation to the other factors appear to be required in the plants—whether there should be substitution of capital for labour or *vice versa.* And the rate of interest may be modified in accordance with any general result which emerges; always raising it if there appears to be an expansive tendency of all plants taken together, and lowering it in the opposite case.

RENTS AND MANAGEMENT.—These present less difficulty: whenever two plants with similar equipment show marked differences in their costs, this must be due either to differences in the ability of the managers or to differences in the qualities of the natural resources being used. In practice it should not be difficult to know which of these causes is operative in a particular case: presumably the Ministry will have an inspectorate of men accustomed to the industries with which they have to deal, so that it need not be haunted by the fear that it will condemn its managers for inefficiency when their apparent shortcomings are due to indifferent soil, narrow seams of coal, and so on. This is more a question of practice than of theory.

All industries dependent on natural resources will show a range of costs. It will be argued below that whenever this is found there is a presumption in favour of expanding the plants, farms, etc., with the lower costs, diverting resources from those with higher costs. Where marginal costs differ from average ones, these must be used, and it will be found that where natural resources are limited expansion always occurs with rising costs. It will be the aim of the Ministry to secure equal marginal costs everywhere, and these equal to the price of the goods: the existence of surpluses, due to differences in the better situated units between marginal and average costs, must not be taken as indicating the need for expansion. If the cost differences persist as expansion continues, they must be due to differences in managing ability, and the high-cost managers replaced if possible. All these matters will need fuller consideration later, but the theory of the subject is well known and there seems no reason why it should not be applied directly to the case we are discussing, if it is possible to calculate the other and basic costs in the manner we have been considering.

The principles which have to be used for pricing the products produced by scarce natural resources are only suitable where the natural resources can be kept intact: a first charge on the products of farms should be whatever is required in the way of manure, drains, etc., to keep the land "in good heart"; and this corresponds to depreciation in the case of capital. But when the natural resources are in the form of exhaustible deposits, another formula is required; for if only rent as so far calculated is charged, the community will gradually impoverish itself. It must also charge something for royalties, and these should be charged on the product even of the marginal deposits. This additional charge has the twofold purpose of restricting the use of the product and providing a source of additional capital the possession of which will offset the loss of the deposits when they are exhausted.

The exact amount to charge for this purpose is somewhat difficult to decide. The reduction in national income when the deposits are exhausted is the difference between the cost of producing the output from them and the cost of producing a similar annual quantity of the next available substitute: so that the maximum amount to add is a sum which, accumulated at compound interest over the period of exhaustion, will produce this difference. This could be added in a tapering proportion every year, so as to compensate for the increased difficulty of working the deposits as they near their end. But it is reasonable to assume that somewhat cheaper substitutes may be discovered before this happens, while it is probable that the reserves will be underestimated at the beginning, as almost always happens with mineral resources. Thus the Ministry will probably be justified in charging something less than the full amount necessary to avoid all possible changes in price. But it is desirable that the receipts from royalties should be accumulated in addition to any other saving which it has been decided to make, since they are not a source of income which can be counted upon indefinitely.

It will be clear that none of the operations we have been considering can be carried out without a certain amount of cost accounting, and that the procedure outlined requires sufficient intelligence on the part of the managers to secure their co-operation. It is not proposed to discuss the possibilities of obtaining this, as it is a matter of opinion rather than one about which we can reason. It should be pointed out, however, that cost accounting is difficult and unreliable in small undertakings, and especially those which employ only two or three workers. This case will need special attention, as will that of single-unit industries— those where all production takes place in one factory. The treatment just given assumes that a large part of the production of the community takes place in establishments between these two extremes.

CHAPTER VI

PRELIMINARY ORGANISATION

WE have now considered the theoretical solution of the problems of economic calculation in a collectivist state. It is impossible to consider the details of organisation, since these depend on the actual circumstances which may happen to be present should an experiment of the kind envisaged be made. Nevertheless it is now proposed to study the question of the mechanism through which the Ministry of Production might carry out its intentions, taking into consideration whatever experience shows to be probable pitfalls in dealing with economic affairs.

It is a common mistake in considering future states of affairs to assume that there will be an alteration in men's characters as soon as they know that they are working for the community. For this reason it is usually argued by the opponents of Socialist plans that Socialism is impracticable, because it assumes that men are perfectible. It seems well, therefore, to state at this point what assumptions are to be made about the character of the labour force which must carry out production in a Socialist community. It appears to the writer that the following conditions are necessary to the success of the operations to be described, and that if they cannot be secured it cannot be claimed for Socialism that it will be able to direct production in what has been defined in Chapter I as a rational manner; whether or not this is an objection to Socialist states which cannot secure these conditions, depends on the point of view of the individual.[1]

It is necessary that the Ministry of Production should be given a free hand in the details of organisation, in the sense that political pressure should not be brought to bear on it except in matters of policy; that it should be in the position of a semi-public concern such as the London Passenger Transport Board rather than a Government department like the Post Office. Second, the Ministry must be able to secure the services of men of a reasonable degree of competence and honesty, such as the members of the administrative grade of the Civil Service of Great Britain: if the first condition can be secured, there should be little difficulty in devising a system of recruitment

[1] For the opposite point of view, cf. Dobb, *Economic Journal*, Dec. 1933.

which will secure men of the necessary character and ability, and in offering them security of tenure and whatever inducement is found necessary to persuade them to work efficiently. Thirdly, the men responsible for the actual conduct of the producing and distributing units must understand the outlines of the methods being employed so that they can provide their costing clerks with information which is in accordance with what is actually going on. The capitalist system finds no difficulty in obtaining managers who do satisfactory work although not shareholders, so that there cannot be any inherent difficulty about Socialism in this respect.

Let us now consider the kind of methods which will be followed. A position of equilibrium can be reached from any beginnings whatever, but in the interests of the community it is preferable to reach it in as short a time as possible (since this is the position of maximum production): serious mistakes in the initial stages might cause much hardship, as is obvious from the experience of Russia. The first task of the Ministry is to place some goods on the market in order to discover the preferences of the consumers. It could assume some sort of *per capita* demand for various goods and try to work out how much could be produced;

101

no doubt after several trial orders of urgency it could make an allocation of the productive resources which would just use them all.

But if, as is likely, the Socialist state succeeds by an evolutionary or revolutionary process some more or less capitalistic system, its task is much simplified. For although incomes will be different (almost certainly more even) and productivity will be different (almost certainly smaller in the earlier stages), the prices previously existing both of goods and of agents of production are likely to be a far better indication of consumers' preferences and of derived costs than any calculations which could be made in an office, however competent its personnel. The variety of consumers' goods might well be simplified, since the small differences in character which are the results of competitive attempts to give individuality to similar products, would lose nearly all their significance if there were no competitive advertising. Such enterprises as supply very expensive articles would be abandoned, since no-one would have a large enough income to be able to buy them; and certain enterprises which exist only because of competition—for example, most kinds of advertising—would also be given up. But apart from these obvious cases, it would be of great advantage to know the kinds of things which had been actually wanted, and the quantities in which they had been actually consumed, by the existing population, whose habits will not be changed overnight because of a change of Government. In the same way, it would be advantageous to know the relative valuations which had been put on the factors of production, since this must be fairly close to the true marginal products of the factors, except in the case of the rate of interest which is affected by monetary conditions more than the prices of labour and natural resources.[1]

The Ministry might try to draw up tentative demand and supply schedules and, by balancing them against one another, finally hit on an allocation of productive resources which would cause all the goods to be sold at their costs of production if the assumed data turned out to be right. But it is probable that it would make serious errors if it did so, especially in the allocation of particular resources to particular tasks. Once the productive processes have

---

[1] N. Kaldor in a review of Dr. Landauer's book, *Planwirtschaft und Verkehrwirtschaft*, says: "No one can regard as anything more than a *naïveté* Dr. Landauer's other idea that the Socialist State should impute at first to the factors of production the same values which were imputed to them under Capitalism" (*Economic Journal*, June 1932, p. 280). Naïveté seems an unduly strong word for a process which, however erroneous, would be extremely useful. The Socialist state must start somewhere.

begun, the resources will begin to be specialised immediately, and errors originally made will be difficult to correct. The capacities of the factors of production, which are usually assumed to be known in economic discussions, vary considerably according to the use which is made of them; but the competitive system tends to draft each factor into that occupation for which it is most suited. If we were faced with an assemblage of machines and labourers and no-one knew the purposes for which they had been made or trained, the results of setting them to work would be chaotic.

It is probable that technical knowledge will be available for the existing machinery, since machines and factories are constructed for some definite purpose, and unless all the engineers are killed or driven out they will be available for consultation. In the light of the dependence of Russia on foreign technicians to tell their own labourers how to make and use machinery, it seems unlikely that any other country embarking on a Socialist experiment will be careless in this matter. There is the same question of specialisation about the labour force. Probably most men can be trained to do most things, although we should not underestimate the differences in innate ability which exist even among the less skilled grades of labour.[1] Whatever our innate capacities, we do need training, and if men have been trained already, they should be kept in positions in which this can be used. These considerations seem very obvious, but we are inclined to take our economic system for granted and to assume that another would begin with all the advantages which exist already: these are the result of a long period of adjustment and of delicate adaptation to the work required.

Apart, therefore, from the simplifications already suggested (less variety and less luxury products), the most sensible course appears to be to keep everyone at the work which they were previously doing, for they would then be using their acquired capacities and producing goods which people had previously wanted in the proportions in which they wanted them. Let us assume, therefore, that the first step is to try to get everybody into their old occupations or, better still, to avoid any dislocation of the work of production at all.[2]

If there has been any dislocation of the economic structure, the next step will be to get

[1] See, for example, the reports on vocational selection of the National Institute of Industrial Psychology.

[2] From a practical point of view this will be difficult without the co-operation of the owners of such businesses as are not managed by employees. From the economic side, a gradual evolution makes calculation much easier than a revolution.

the plant running, and this will require a period of saving during which the community will only receive whatever is necessary to keep them in health. For whether it is proposed to make any annual saving or not, before the community can begin to consume the products of its enterprises it must accumulate all the intermediate products which are needed for a continuous flow of production. Before any final product can be placed on the market, work has to be carried out on a number of stages: thus, work must be begun almost a year before bread is ready to eat; and all this time the product is moving forward, so to speak, carrying more and more labour which is expended on it as it passes from ploughed land to growing crop, and so to wheat, to flour, and to the baker's counter. The community has to acquire a stock of goods in all stages of production, so that everyone can work steadily, at whatever stage of the process he is employed. In the same way, whatever work is necessary to recondition the machinery must be expended. Thus the smoother the transition from the previous régime the better; the ideal change would involve no previous break, so that all the working capital previously accumulated would be available for the new system. But it is unlikely that this could be done, and to the extent that there had been losses there would be a period of forced saving when production exceeded consumption.

If everything had been destroyed, the problem would be much more complex. In the first place, the community would have no time to wait, and would have to choose the most rapid processes possible in order to obtain food to survive. When they had done this, they would have open to them a large variety of possible productivities according to the period which they were prepared to wait while they accumulated the necessary capital. But the view taken here is that the problem can be treated much more simply. Provided that the community can feed themselves at all, there will be processes available because they had been previously in use, and in general these will be the ones chosen. Now *once they are chosen,* each requires that amount of working capital, and therefore that amount of *original* saving, which its technical methods involve. There is then no question of the period of production, or of how many intermediate products may be used; for if you are to use the process at all, you must wait for a known period and, after this, only need to keep the capital intact. The question of savings other than this initial amount will be considered later.

If this policy is adopted, the Ministry of Production will soon begin to accumulate stocks of finished goods and the population can now become consumers. To do this they must be given incomes, and it is important that they should have been kept to rations during the period of saving, as otherwise they would have accumulated purchasing power. What is needed is that they should have a steady flow of incomes, corresponding to the available amounts of goods.

In a capitalist society the equation of prices and incomes occurs automatically, since all prices paid for goods are distributed in the form of wages, profits, interests, and rent. If there is no inflation going on, no income is available except in this way or through gifts or taxation from the classes who receive the wages, etc., and their incomes are reduced by the amounts of their gifts or taxes. If there is no hoarding of money, the total incomes are spent and provide funds for the purchase of the goods and the payment of incomes in the succeeding period. In the Socialist state, which owns all the land and capital and performs all the functions which enable the entrepreneur to make profits, there are no outgoings corresponding to profits, interest, or rent. And there is no necessity to distribute anything as wages

108

either, since all payments might be made without reference to the work performed. But it is probable that in the interests of efficiency most of the incomes will be paid in the form of wages and that there will be some differences in wage payments to different classes of workers.

On this assumption, payments may now be classified as follows:

(a) Wages to workers in public departments (police, education, army, etc.).

(b) Payments for material to be used by these departments. It is essential that they should pay for what they use in order to control the allocation to them.

(c) Wages to workers in general, including those who will make good depreciation and construct new capital goods, if any.

(d) Other incomes. In this category will appear sums paid, whether in money or in kind, to the old, the infirm, and anyone else who is not going to work but to whom it is desired to give an income.

There will also be payments from each undertaking to those others from which it purchases its raw material, or the semi-finished goods which it uses as raw material. But these payments will not affect the demand for finished goods; they will need consideration in connection with monetary policy, which will be discussed later.

Some Socialists hope that every individual will receive the same income; others that payments will be made according to need—"to each according to his necessity". It is improbable that anyone will succeed in devising a formula for ascertaining need which would be generally acceptable: the most that is likely would be some extra allowances for illness and for families. If either equality or some other precise scale were adopted, all the classes of payments except (b) could be added up easily. It has already been stated that it is unlikely that efficient work will be done unless more is paid for it than for inefficient. It will be suggested later that everyone should be paid the amount necessary to make him work efficiently. There will be a surplus available, since the prices charged for goods will include charges for interest and rent and there is no-one to receive these amounts automatically as in a capitalist state. From this surplus, incomes of class (d) will be paid in accordance with whatever scale is thought expedient; and also the payments for material to be used for (b) and for new capital goods. Since differences of income, rather than absolute amounts, determine to a large extent the efficiency of workers, the whole income scale may be moved up or down in order to provide whatever sums are necessary for state services and for new savings. If, however, there is anything over after payments have been made as suggested, there could be an equal increase of everyone's income.

At present, the exact form of income distribution is immaterial. When something has been decided, money can be printed or coined to the required amount: what is needed is enough to keep up the weekly or monthly payments until enough has been received from the sales of goods to establish a regular flow. The amounts paid should not at first be varied, though of course the first form of income distribution can be modified later in accordance with experience or change of policy. The monetary unit is of no consequence, but the more like the previous one it is the less disturbance of mental habits will there be; while if the tentative prices have been formed from past experience, the size of incomes will also be like those previously received. The distributive agencies, shops in fact, can then be opened.

The goods must be priced in accordance with two considerations. First, their relative prices must correspond to whatever estimates of cost have been made by the Ministry;

second, the total price of all the goods must be equal to or greater than the total of incomes plus expenditure of public services on material. Except in the case of perishable goods, it is desirable to price the goods slightly higher than the total amount which is available to spend on them: this will allow stocks to be accumulated and give security to the system, and it is better that the consumers should find goods to the extent of their incomes rather than have nothing on which to spend them. The market is not likely to be cleared exactly by the original prices, and any deficiency of purchases because the consumers did not want the goods will mean that something else runs short and will have to be rationed until the prices are raised, unless there are stocks in hand. And any form of rationing is inequitable; if it is desired to mark differences between different classes, as has been done in Russia, it is much more reasonable to do it by means of income differences than by interfering with the pricing mechanism.

As soon as purchases begin, it will be found that the prices are wrong owing to the conjectural nature of the original data. Some goods will be bought faster than they are being made, while stocks of others are piling up. It is now necessary to collect information about these

movements of stocks, an easy matter to anyone accustomed to the operations of chain
stores. No doubt local tastes will admit of some
cancellation, stocks of tea accumulating in
town A and of coffee in town B being transferred. But it is certain that the whole market
will not be cleared, and it is now necessary to
adjust the prices of goods, raising the prices
of those for which the amount demanded is
greater than the supply, and lowering them in
the opposite case. It has already been explained
that the effect of price-changes is to alter the
relative attractiveness of goods, restricting or
enlarging the demands; and it is clear that some
set of prices can be found which will just get
rid of the goods at the rate at which they are
coming in. Perhaps if the Ministry were badly
in the dark at the beginning, some goods will
have been made which will not be taken at all.
Any large enterprises which make such things
should have been closed already if there has
been a reasonable degree of foresight (the enterprises already referred to which make luxury
goods, etc.); but it seems probable that a number of individuals and small enterprises will
find themselves left out of the original plan.
Any resources producing goods for which there
is no demand at all should be stopped at once
and transferred to the production of anything

113

which has a price; though the higher this price over the estimated cost (if this has been estimated) the better. At first no other production should be altered, the aim being to find the prices which will dispose of the existing output.

The Ministry has now established a continuous flow of goods to the consumer, the amount depending on the efficiency with which it has been able to organise production on the lines previously followed. The receipts will be forwarded through the banking system, presumably, to the distributing centres in order to pay the incomes. If it is found convenient, producing centres might be given the receipts in order to pay the wages, but since these do not correspond in any particular place to the receipts there, a general collection and redistribution is necessary. If any money is hoarded, fresh amounts must be manufactured in order to maintain income payments, and if dishoarding takes place the surplus will be stored or destroyed.

The community are now getting the best use possible from the *available goods*, on the assumption that this occurs when those who want things most are getting them. If the goods were forthcoming in the existing proportions as a result of fixed causes, instead of the proceedings of the Ministry, the best prices are those which clear the market. Variations in taste will express themselves in changing prices, but in the absence of competitive advertising it is reasonable to suppose that demand will be fairly stable; we should expect small price variations once the initial stages have been passed, and the various people concerned in collecting information and adjusting prices should soon become efficient at this work, which must be done continuously during the next stage, that of adjusting prices to costs. This will express itself in changes in the supplies of goods, and prices should be moved continuously as stocks alter, the aim being always to find prices which will clear the market at the same rate as that at which goods come from the producers.

CHAPTER VII

EQUATION OF PRICES AND COSTS

IT has been observed above that it should be the aim of the Ministry to sell the goods at their marginal costs and to find these costs from the productivity of the factors of production. This involves a process of successive approximation, and not a vicious circle. It is this process which must now be undertaken, along the lines indicated in Chapter V.

Except in special cases, where all production of a commodity takes place in one enterprise, the productive units will either have equal costs or different ones; more probably the latter. If we range the different costs in order from the least to the greatest, then we have by construction a range over which costs increase, and this is the typical case. Since the loss to the community from producing the most expensive unit is the amount which the factors of production there employed could produce elsewhere, it is this price which must be used in calculation; if we charged average cost, the community would get the last units at less than

116

cost, and would be induced by the lower price to buy more of this good and therefore less of some other, which it would have preferred if the prices had been equal, and which could have been produced at the same expenditure of resources. We shall therefore aim at adjusting prices to marginal costs and use the concept of rent; the Ministry must charge rents for those resources which are more productive than the last which must be used. The method of marginal productivity allows the comparison of similar resources used in different fields of production.

The first step will be to place some figure on what are considered to be the various grades of labour, and to assume values for the working capital and for the rate of interest. The rates previously existing will be the most useful guide towards fixing the price of capital, using, as has been said, some average of long-term rates rather than of short-term ones. With regard to labour, it is well known that the expense of training and the accident of social advantages cause deviations of the actual wages in a capitalist state from what is considered the best figure from the point of view adopted here. The activities of trade and professional organisations also introduce monopolist elements into wages, so that to assume

117

labour costs to be what they were before is an unjustified proceeding. On the other hand, all specialised labour will be about as scarce in relation to demand as it was before, so that we cannot assume at once that labour is available for particular uses because we have put it into a grade. The problem will be quantitatively different in a country where mass production is common and labour can be trained easily from one where special skill is usual. Probably the old rates will be the best guide, if they are somewhat corrected for anomalies of a monopolistic appearance; men who are accustomed to industry can usually tell fairly closely when these are present.[1]

It is possible either to neglect the value of the fixed capital or to assume some figure for it also, the difficulty being that it is desirable to use it until it is worn out, even if it is not returning its assumed value. The value of land and of specialised plant depends on what it can earn and not on what it cost to improve or produce. It seems preferable to make estimates of the cost of replacement of all fixed capital, as it is important to make provision for depreciation; the price to be placed on land will have to be deduced later, and it must be

[1] Cf. Marshall's remarks on his own ability in this respect. Preface to *Industry and Trade*.

remembered that the fixed capital of least efficiency will not be expected to earn interest or depreciation. The original estimates of cost will be inaccurate both in detail because of ignorance, and probably in general in the sense that they may all be too high or too low because it is difficult to estimate exactly the average level of costs which will correspond to the amount of money which has been placed in circulation.

Let us consider the second point. The aim of the Ministry is to equate prices and marginal costs, which is to be done by varying the amounts of the various goods. But if the price-level is fixed by the weekly stream of incomes, there will be only one general level of costs which will employ all the labour and such of the capital and land as is warranted by the complex of data which affect the price system. If the original estimates of costs are too high there will appear to be a case for not employing all the resources; if too low, it will seem desirable to expand all production, and though this cannot be done, the relative changes required may be masked to some extent. The Ministry must be prepared for these contingencies: as downward changes in money income are unpopular, it is more likely to change the level of costs when action is necessary. We

119

have observed that such discrepancies will be a useful guide to the rate of interest; an index of labour costs might also be constructed and the component parts modified if there is any tendency to unemployment or over-employment. The value of capital will be calculated from labour costs and interest rates by the capital constructing industries, and modified automatically as these change.

If these changes are made whenever necessary, the way is clear for an adjustment of production: production of goods showing a surplus of price over cost being expanded; production not covering interest and depreciation being kept steady, and the remainder contracted. This will involve transfers of resources from the last to the first group of productive units. In a few cases this will be simple: thus, fairly wide changes in agricultural products can be made, wheat land being put to vegetables or oats or pastures; the colours or shapes of garments can be changed; and so on. The characteristic of such changes will be that the increase in production takes place at about the same costs as before. But when the transfer has to take place between disparate industries, this will not be true; costs will rise steeply as production increases, owing to the alteration in form of the capital and in training of the workers, which is necessary before the costs can be similar. A surplus of farms and farm labourers does not help much towards an expansion of electrical supplies.

At the end of this process of adjustment, the Ministry will be selling all its products at their marginal costs; but in some cases there will be a marked difference between these costs and the average ones. There will be a marked improvement in the production of the goods where there has been transfer of similar resources, and prices have fallen or risen towards costs; but in most cases we may expect that expansion of production will have been checked by rising costs rather than by a change in the price due to increased output.

It is now necessary to carry out several adjustments at the same time, though we must treat them seriatim. The success with which they can be done depends on the ability of the people in charge of the factories or plants, and in particular on their ability to distinguish three possible causes of high or low costs, which may be due to differences in the fixed plant or land, to differences in management, or to differences in the quality of the labour. The writer has already given his opinion that these matters are capable of judgement by men who are accustomed to the branch of production in question, and that unless such men flatly refuse to work for a socialist community the difficulties will not be insuperable.

Consider the aspect of the rising costs which were present, no doubt, before adjustment began, but have been accentuated by the attempt to expand with unsuitable resources. Since the high cost units are producing at cost, the low cost ones are earning profits or efficiency-rents, an expression of the estimate of the community of the value of the superior plant. An examination of these rents will reveal curious results, more particularly where they include charges for the skill of some workers whose rivals at the margin are not so skilled. Suppose, for example, that doctors are scarce and (an unlikely supposition) that their services are priced in order to restrict the demand on them, but that they are rated at some general figure for professional labour. Any attempt to draft in fresh labour will be defeated by the incompetence of the newcomers, whose receipts, if anything, will be small, so that soon they will only equal the rated figure. The surgeries of the trained men will appear to be earning large efficiency-rents, but if similar ones are constructed they will fail in their purpose because there are still no more doctors: there is nothing for it but to rate them at the figure derived from their earnings. This absurd example illustrates what will really happen in numerous cases.

Now, whenever this happens, and expansion is checked by rising costs, there must be present either a difference between natural resources and innate abilities, in which case there is a true rent present or a shortage of training or of properly adapted capital, in which case the term efficiency rent has been used. If biscuits are in great demand, then their production will be extended until they are being produced by ordinary cooks on ordinary stoves, at the point where their price just covers their cost. The biscuit factories will be showing large efficiency-rents, which would be profits in a capitalist community. This would there lead to the expansion of the factories, either from the investment of the accumulated profits or through the investment of savings being made elsewhere, the production of factory biscuits being extended until the price had fallen and the profits were eliminated.

The next task is to expand the plants earning efficiency-rents, and this could be done by earmarking anything which they produced above their own costs, including depreciation for their own expansion through new construction or through training new workers specialised

123

for their own type of work. It can be laid down as a general principle that whenever there is a surplus of receipts over interest and depreciation, the first claim on it should be for financing expansion of this kind. But at this point a decision is needed about the rate of saving.

If the habits of the consumers have not changed much, so that the original scheme of production, which closely resembles that previously existing, also resembles closely what is to be the result of all the adjustments; that is, if the adjustments required are small, then there is little difficulty. But if large changes in the form of the productive equipment are needed, then the question arises as to how fast they are to be carried out. For if every unit with a large surplus expands out of that surplus, there will be two effects which need consideration: the reduction of the incomes of the community during the expansion, and the development of large capacity in the industries which make capital goods, which capacity will be too large after the work of adjustment has been carried out. The effects will be similar to those of a boom in a capitalist state; in that case the extra capacity is due to monetary expansion, while here it is due to the decision to save at a faster rate than it is intended to maintain.

124

Some arbitrary decision must be made in the light of these considerations: any community which has its resources seriously misplaced must endure the pains of reconstruction. There is no index by which it can be decided that one rate of saving is better than another, since we are allowing for the future and can only guess about the data required for a decision. No content can be given to the idea of an optimum in this connection, and the decision is a political rather than an economic one. In Chapter V the case in which it was decided to keep the size of the industries producing capital goods fixed was treated. Whatever the decision, the procedure will be much the same if the demand for expansion is greater than these industries can meet at once; the rate of interest and the price of capital goods will be raised in order to restrict the pace of expansion, and the high price of capital goods will not be allowed to cause an expansion of the industries producing them beyond the point which has been agreed upon.

Apart from this limitation, the principle of allowing units producing a surplus to use this for expansion should be followed, and this will cause a change in the amounts produced, more or less gradual according to the decision about saving, until finally it will be impossible to use the surpluses so that they will produce more surpluses, either because prices have fallen or because marginal costs have risen. At this point any remaining surpluses are rents which cannot be reduced, and can be diverted to incomes or to any kind of other purpose which is considered expedient. The new plants may be better than the old and themselves produce surpluses; in which case the first plants will be closed as they depreciate and the new plants gradually become the standard. At the end of all this adjustment, every branch of production should be showing either constant or increasing costs, so that all plants will have been brought to as efficient a state as is possible with the existing knowledge on the subject. There will be no such thing as decreasing costs in the sense that as production expands costs continue to fall, except in those industries where only one plant remains. These we shall consider later.

In the meantime, the process of checking the assumed costs must be going on. The managers of the different plants which are expanding, owing to the fact that they are more than covering their costs, will be instructed to do so with any modifications in the relative proportions of the factors of production which may give lower costs. In order to do this, they

126

will be forced to estimate the marginal productivities of the factors which they employ. It would be a mistake to make any direct use of these calculations to modify the costs, with which the Ministry is working, since no particular man or unit of capital will actually be situated at the ideal margin. But if the process of expansion, which is accompanied by a process of contraction elsewhere, leads to a change in the relative demands for factors, clearly their assumed prices must have been wrong: the Ministry must use these estimates in order to check their figures for the different grades of labour as a whole, and for capital in general. If it appears that the price of some grade of labour, for example, is rising because industry finds it leads to lower costs to use more of it, and it is possible to train more of this labour from the material of other grades less in demand, then this should be begun immediately. It seems that there should be two successive changes in the cost figure for this labour: first charging it at a high rate to restrict its use, and then lowering its price again after new men have been trained. This would lead to some dislocation, because the first arrangements would be made for a price which was not going to continue; however, the figures might be "cooked" somewhat if it were thought that

127

this would reduce the dislocation.

The efficiency with which the operations described above can be carried out depends on whether the Ministry can supply its own managers both with correct figures of their sales results—which should be easy—and with suitable figures of costs to be used in order to find out whether expansion or contraction is necessary. At the works end, the managers will need to be capable of using these cost figures and of ascertaining roughly the marginal contributions of their resources; and they must have some inducement to keep their costs down. The whole practicability of Socialism depends on whether a suitable personnel can be obtained, a matter on which no dogmatic pronouncements should be made. There are, however, several remarks which may be made.

The prices obtainable from the consumers are the only figures which are provided automatically. The others are fixed by the Ministry from the use of index figures, the result of information which they themselves collect. But the criteria on which action must be taken are quite simple, and there does not appear to be any difficulty about using them. In the actual fixing of costs there will be most diversity about labour costs, and it might well be advantageous to sacrifice some accuracy to simplicity,

EQUATION OF PRICES AND COSTS

grouping the labour into a comparatively small number of classes. As long as mistakes will be more likely to be found out the worse they are, the results cannot be bad, and it will be easier for the costing arrangements in the actual works if the figures are fairly simple. At first it may appear strange that there are no actual receipts or payments, but all large businesses work mainly through banks and it is easy to become accustomed to working to figures on paper. Since these are supplied from an external source, they cannot be manipulated for long, any more than can those of, for example, the branches of a large bank.

Is there any way of ensuring that the managers themselves are efficient? We have already remarked that there is some danger of confusing rents due to efficiency with those due to superior circumstances, such as better sites or soil. The procedure we have laid down is that of arranging all the units in order of cost, and attributing differences in output to differences in circumstances. Every unit, if properly conducted, will extend its operations to the point where the marginal cost equals the price which is received: the intensive margin will be the same as the extensive one. But in better placed units, average cost will not be the same as marginal.

The optimum production takes place when it all occurs at the point of minimum average cost, and, where the plant is being duplicated out of the surpluses received, this will tend to happen, all units finally producing at the same cost. But where there is a true rent, each unit will have cost curves peculiar to itself; expansion cannot occur at costs as low as are obtaining elsewhere because the best resources are already occupied. Now the question arises, can we differentiate between high costs due to inefficient management and those due to scarce resources? If, for example, two farms have different costs, can we say that it is a proper state of affairs because there is a difference in the soils, or an improper one because of the difference in the farmers?

The method of making extension of output the first claim on surpluses, while allowing plant which is not covering interest on its cost to depreciate until worn out, will of itself allow the problems of efficiency and of size to solve themselves to some extent. For the more efficient the manager, the larger will his accounting surplus become; and if he is encouraged to expand his own works, the larger also will it be, at the expense of the resources which other managers are not employing so well. As the general level of management improves, the prices attributed to the factors of production will rise and make it more difficult for the less efficient to carry on. And if there is really some size of undertaking which can produce at lower cost than any other, it is this one which will establish itself.

It is more probable that the capacity to manage works efficiently is scarce, and that the quantity of resources which can be controlled effectively by one man is limited. If this is so, an end will be reached of any individual expansion, and subsequent attempts to expand will have to be made with the men of inferior capacity. Thus costs of the new plants will be above the average, though not the marginal, costs of the old; and the surpluses will have to be considered as true rents, in the sense that they cannot be avoided with the given scarcity of talent. But in the interests of the community it is desirable that these should be as small as possible and that the Ministry should know exactly how much of its cost difference are due to human shortcomings.

The matter of inducements to the managers will be discussed when we are dealing with incomes. In a capitalist community individuals are encouraged to be efficient by the prospect of obtaining for themselves any payments which arise because of their superiority over others; and the competition for productive resources keeps up their price, so that only those who can make effective use of them can secure them. Here we are concerned with whether the Ministry can find out how its own managers compare with one another.

Experimentally this could be done by the method of substitution: by exchanging the managers of two units which are working at different cost levels, and thus isolating the other possible causes. For if two men operate successively the same plant, the difference of result must be due to their own differences. But this method is not convenient, owing to the time lag—the period during which a man is becoming accustomed to new conditions and personnel. The method of expert supervision seems to be preferable. It is a matter of observation that men who have been trained to a business and have themselves been successful in it, will become capable of estimating quite closely the capacities of particular concerns. For example, land agents and valuers can judge quite accurately the rental value of farms without working them themselves; and all large businesses employ the same methods. Further, there is no reason why the Socialist state should conceal anything about its productive methods, so that it should be possible to help backward managers by information and by allowing them to observe directly the methods of the more successful ones. In modern capitalist countries there is a special class of firms who give advice of this kind—efficiency experts—and it would be advantageous to the Ministry of Production to take over all such concerns directly. We may conclude, then, that the Ministry will have methods open to it by which it may discover the qualities of its managers.

With the accomplishment of this step, the community will be in working order; having a steady production of goods which are being sold to the consumers, and the output of which is constantly varied as the processes of cost determination become more accurate. And at the same time constant endeavours will be made to replace high cost plants by those with lower costs, so that the final position will be that of constant or unavoidably increasing costs.

CHAPTER VIII

LARGE AND SMALL PRODUCTIVE UNITS

WE must now consider two special cases. The organisation of production so far considered as typical is that of a number of units, each of fairly large size, which are engaged in the same lines of production: not the same product, since few products are made by any concern to the exclusion of all others; but the same range, with the same factors of production, so that the comparison of costs is possible. There are two types of productive unit which do not conform to that used in the analysis so far made. These are the very large and the very small unit, the first because no comparison can be made and the second because the costing operations are likely to be expensive and unreliable.

Let us consider as the type of the large unit a productive organisation which makes the whole of a certain class of products, since this is the most difficult case: the more there are the easier does the solution become. Professor Hayek, in his second essay in the work already mentioned, suggests that this will be the typical case.[1] He argues that this will present an insuperable obstacle, adducing the well-known passage from Edgeworth's discussion of monopolies in support of this view. In a world of monopolies, says Edgeworth, there is no determinate equilibrium: "there would survive only the empirical school, flourishing in the chaos congenial to their mentality". Now it is probable that, in a world of monopolies, prices are likely to be unstable, including those of the factors of production. What will happen depends on the extent to which the monopolists allow for the reactions of the other monopolists to their actions, and this behaviour cannot be predicted. But as far as the Socialist state is concerned, this theoretical difficulty is one which does not arise, and Professor Hayek introduces Edgeworth's analysis in a situation to which it is quite inapplicable. Edgeworth was considering a condition in which all the monopolies were competing for the customers with the aim of making as large profits as possible for themselves. It is certain that no Socialist would suppose that there is anything socialist about such a state of affairs: the aim is not to "exploit the consumer", in Professor Hayek's words,[2] but to make the

---

[1] *Collectivist Economic Planning,* pp. 220-222.
[2] *Op. cit.* p. 222.

THE ECONOMIC SYSTEM IN A SOCIALIST STATE

best use of resources. And the reaching of equilibrium is theoretically much easier when there is an attempt to equate prices and marginal costs than it is when the attempt is to maximise profits. When we add that the Ministry is also attempting to compare the efficiency of factors, measured by the values they produce, in different industries, all indeterminateness is removed.

The extent to which this form of organisation will occur is doubtful, but there is no *prima facie* reason why it should predominate: the economies of large-scale production, as Professor Hayek remarks himself in the section which follows that with which we have just dealt, soon come to an end in many cases. It is true that in the Socialist state all production will be directed by the Ministry of Production, and presumably particular branches of production will be grouped into departments which control the units producing similar types of goods, so that in a formal sense all production is controlled by one agency. But if the sub-department is trying to compare its units as we have suggested that it should, this is no disadvantage. The work of comparison will be positively facilitated by the fact that supervision takes place from a central headquarters.

The number of single unit productive concerns in England is very small. In Germany,
the home of monopolies, it is significant that
the cartel is the typical form of organisation,
with the productive units retaining their own
individuality. The best-known American trusts
have either a number of producing centres, or
have to compete with smaller independent
units, or both. At first sight public utilities
appear to be examples of unified control, but
often this is not really so. The supply of gas,
water, sewerage, and so on, is peculiarly suited
to comparison, for we have a large number of
independent undertakings whose results can
be compared with ease by an inspectorate. If
the most successful managers of such undertakings are promoted to the central directing body, they should have no difficulty in
imposing common standards of costing and,
through these, of performance. The relations
of bodies like the Board of Education with
municipal schools in England are instructive
in this respect. It is true that all such bodies
are bureaucratic, and indeed the whole organisation which we have been discussing is bureaucratic. The Ministry of Production will not be
bankrupted if it is slack in its work; it is obvious
that if it is corrupt or inefficient the whole
organisation will function badly. But we have

137

already stated that unless it can command the services of men who are honest and capable our plans will be unworkable, so that we have so far introduced no new difficulty.

There remain undertakings, of which perhaps the Central Electricity Board in England is an example—and perhaps the main transport system would also be one if it were unified—in which the operations are really carried out as a whole. We might add that in a backward or small community there might be a large number of these, as the optimum size of unit might easily be capable of supplying the whole needs of the community. For this reason small or isolated Socialist states will have special difficulties from lack of comparative data.

The problem in such cases is insoluble for all communities, collectivist, capitalist, or corporative. If a single productive unit is more efficient than a number of small units, how can we tell whether it is as efficient as it might be? It has already passed and eliminated its competitors. If a world champion has no-one against which to measure himself, how can he tell of what he is capable? A runner can run against himself by means of a stop-watch: will a state concern be prepared to make continuous efforts to reduce its own costs? If it does not do so, no-one else can. In a capitalist state Nemesis is always waiting for the lethargic monopoly, as the calamity of the internal combustion engine fell upon the railways. But it is doubtful whether anyone in a collectivist state would have any hope of starting a rival department to something like the state telephone service.

If there are other states, a comparison becomes possible: it would be to the advantage of Socialist states to collaborate, and the only example which we have at present, Russia, seems anxious to learn from capitalist states. If this is impossible, then we must admit the difficulty; it does seem to be true that as the controllers of an unassailable monopoly grow old, the machinery which they control loses its adaptability and routine methods appear; those in charge are able to set up a successful resistance to would-be innovators. The difficulty is much the same as that which is found in attempting to introduce promotion by merit in the Civil Service. But if the Ministry is aware that it is likely to occur, so that it looks with especial interest on any units of this kind, there is little danger of large losses; and particularly if it keeps a staff of efficiency experts, who are encouraged to criticise the administration of any organisation which appears to be too satisfied with its own performances.

The case of small units is quite different. In

capitalist societies individuals of an enterprising disposition are constantly watching for opportunities of supplying some good or service in a cheaper or better way than is being done before their appearance. If they are successful and establish themselves, their businesses may develop and finally become large ones, and themselves the pioneers of new industries. We shall discuss later the question of research and innovation in a Socialist state, but it seems doubtful whether opportunities for such developments will be present, particularly if the fundamental condition is to be that there is no private ownership of the means of production.

But there is another class of small unit which will always remain small. This is due to the geographical dispersion of population over the surface of the earth: in Adam Smith's expression, the division of labour is limited by the extent of the market. It does not pay to have large units to supply a scattered population, because of the cost of transporting the goods and services to the point where they will be used. Although with the cheapening of transport this becomes less important, it seems that there will always be room for small units if only because of the convenience to the consumers of being able to see what is available and to give personal instructions. We should not underestimate the advantages to be derived from the opportunities of personal contact in this way, even where the difference in cost in favour of the large unit is considerable. It cannot be measured exactly, but the persistence of small establishments in the face of lower prices and apparently better service from large ones, is a marked feature of the competitive world. And since the aim of the Ministry is to make the best use of resources, we must not neglect the question because of accounting difficulties.

Any village and most suburbs present obvious examples of what is meant. The small shop "round the corner", the odd-job man, the village blacksmith or barber, chimney-sweeps, window-cleaners—everyone can call to mind favourite examples. All these things can be done by the employees of large establishments, and the chain store gives us an example of successful standardisation, but it is most successful where the population is comparatively dense. The chain store gets its low costs from various circumstances, almost all of which depend for their occurrence on a large turnover; and this is unobtainable with a scattered people.

There are no theoretical difficulties about costing and pricing for one individual supplier except those which arise from discontinuity, *i.e.* from the fact that purchases are made in finite amounts and a man's time cannot be subdivided beyond a certain extent, so that the calculations of cost become rough ones. But from the practical point of view we can hardly expect the individual worker, or the manager of one or two workers, to be capable of using a costing system in a way which will make the results mean anything. It is difficult enough in a large works to get the hands to give an account of how they have spent their time which will allow of the accurate costing of jobs. No system of control can be expected to work when the responsible persons are not capable of doing what is required of them, and it would be wasteful to place men who could do such work in positions of little importance.

Nor is it of any use to proceed by means of inspectors who will go through the accounts of the managers of small units and proceed against the inefficient, negligent, or dishonest among them. For if the difficulty is the lack of men it will only be accentuated by getting rid of some of them.

Further, it would be necessary to make such units proceed on fixed lines if they are to be controlled, and if they are to get the advantages of standardisation. But when a man has a variety of different things to attend to he is likely to waste a good deal of time owing to the requirements of a fixed routine: it is this which makes the procedure of Government servants in small offices sometimes so irritating; as, for example, in small post offices in France. The man who is to perform managerial functions, wherever he is, must have freedom for his decisions, which are often the result of a mental process which he would find it hard to explain.

In the competitive world, where the owners of small establishments have financial responsibility, there is no difficulty. Each can keep what books he chooses in his own way, and arrange his time according to the situation of the moment; he acquires some sort of practical judgement which allows him to make more or less correct decisions even if he could not give a reasonable explanation of them. And the unsuccessful are weeded out because they cannot make ends meet or perhaps through the bankruptcy court, if they wait long enough.

The Socialist state must decide whether it is prepared to modify at all its attitude towards production by the individual; if it is determined that no-one, however insignificant, is to sell anything except through the official machine, then it must either go without whatever advantages are to be derived from small men, or suffer the shortcomings which it is likely to find if it attempts to organise them. It has been said that the Russian planners would have made a large gain in production if they had chosen in an arbitrary way some number less than 10, for example 3, and decreed that anyone who chose would be allowed to employ up to that number of men, but no more; prescribing whatever conditions as to hours and wages it was able to afford its own employees. This would prevent the re-emergence of a capitalist system unless the Socialist one was hopelessly inefficient, in which case it is difficult to justify its continued existence; but would make use of those men, already discussed, who fill the gaps between the main structure of industry and who make their best efforts if left to themselves. In the opinion of the writer there is much to be said for this course for several reasons.

If, in fact, the difficulties of organisation which have been considered here are found to exist, then this method would avoid them. There is no reason why the state enterprises should not compete with these small men if the Ministry sees fit, and the competition thus provided would be an indication to it as to its own progress with any movement comparable

144

to chain stores. As we have said, the value of such services is hard to compute, but it is worth considering.

"It's the little things in life a woman feels, dear," as the charwoman in Mr. A. P. Herbert's poem said; we do not know what we would give for the convenience of having someone whom we knew to be approachable for our odd jobs, because there is nearly always someone available at standard rates.

Finally, it may be observed that there exist at all times individuals who attach great importance to independence. Socialists sometimes seem to have rather contradictory views on this point; while they object strongly to the position of precarious subservience in which the worker is placed by his dependence on the capitalist employer, they do not like the idea of anyone in the Socialist state having a place outside the state mechanism. Those only are to lose their chains who find their freedom in the service of the state as the state is constituted. The persecution of the more successful of the peasants in Russia is difficult to justify unless it is held that independence is in itself a sign of moral obliquity.

Now in any system the men of marked ability and independent outlook will reach positions of responsibility in which they will find congenial employment, unless they live under an arbitrary despotism. There is no such thing as equality among people of different abilities, since leaders will always be necessary and it is unavoidable that they should be marked off in some way. The majority of men seem to prefer to be subject to some discipline as a result of which they will not have to be responsible, so that they will fit in well enough in our scheme of organisation: security against loss of income, security against the caprice of those who direct them, are the essentials on the immaterial side of their employment. But there seems to be little room for the independently minded man of mediocre ability; and if this can be found by allowing him to become a capitalist in a small way, and at the same time a gap in the economic arrangements is filled, there is a gain on both sides. The arbitrary limit to the extension of such operations will mean that the more able men will find more attractive openings in the field of state-controlled industry: thus there will be no danger of encouraging a movement which will later destroy the foundations of the state. Socialism which has anything to fear from the small trader must be a poor thing.[1]

[1] For the Russian method of dealing with this problem, see Appendix.

CHAPTER IX

INCOMES

THE absolute size of real incomes, or standard of living, will depend on the productivity of the system. This is governed by circumstances external to the economic arrangements, such as the natural resources, by the efficiency of the Ministry in adjusting prices to costs, and by the efficiency of the productive mechanism. The externally determined situation is a matter of fact in each case, and we cannot forecast the efficiency of the Ministry or its managers, though we have considered the means by which they can find out how they are progressing in this way.

The question now to be considered is that of the relative sizes of incomes: whether they will all be equal and, if not, the principles on which their differences are to be determined; A simple equality of payments is easy enough. after providing for depreciation and new capital and for Government services, the remainder will be divided among those who are to receive incomes. But we should inquire whether this

147

is really equality, and also into the relation between efficiency and income.

The real income of the individual should be considered not only with respect to the purchasing power of the money income, but also to the other circumstances which attend the receipt of the income. If the Ministry sells goods at cost price, the price will vary from place to place according to the cost of transport, and the money incomes must be modified as the price-level, in this case a cost-of-living index, varies. But there will also be differences in attendant advantages: thus many things are obtainable in a large town which cannot be got at all in the country—theatres, restaurants, libraries, and so on. In the country there are other advantages for those who like them, and to many people the climate, which varies from place to place, is of great importance. Finally, it is unlikely that all employments will appear equally attractive to everyone. It might be possible to avoid attaching any social status to any employment, but tastes differ. Some men like to be farmers, others to do repetition work in which they do not have to think, others to occupy responsible posts and to command their fellows. It is inconceivable that tastes should coincide with opportunities, for example that exactly as many men will wish to work with steam-hammers as are needed for such work. But if the Ministry drafts men by force into those occupations in which there is a shortage of labour, or to serve in those parts of its territory which are unpopular, it will not be treating its personnel at all equally merely by seeing that each can purchase about the same basketful of commodities.

It seems, therefore, that equality of net advantages is more likely to be sought than equality of money incomes. This might also involve differences of payment according to family responsibilities, but this point will not be discussed, since it involves the position of the family and of women, a social rather than an economic question. The net advantages, except those dependent on differences in purchasing power, cannot be discovered independently of the opinions of the community, since it is upon these that they depend. We are faced with the same problem as that of discovering what to produce, and must give the same answer: some sort of market must be organised in order to find out what people think.

A labour market means that the worker is free to offer to work anywhere he chooses: the terms of employment are fixed by the Ministry and the worker can accept or reject them, and his income becomes a wage, though it will differ in some respects from the wage under capitalism, it being probable that wage payments will be more equal under a Socialist régime. We shall discuss the important question of the conditions of labour shortly, but at this point it must be remarked that there should be some inducement to make the labourers offer to work: the obvious course is to give no incomes to those who will not work. There should be no unemployment in the sense that there are no jobs for those who are willing to work; it would be gross negligence on the part of the Ministry if this occurred. It is likely that most men are happier if they have something to do, but there are always numbers of individuals who prefer to be idle, and if they are treated as well as those who work there is sure to be discontent and demoralisation of the others. If it is considered that it is too drastic to refuse support altogether to the idlers, it is essential that their treatment should be worse to a marked extent than that of all who work.

In the early stages of organisation, the workers cannot be consulted much about their tastes: as has been seen, it is probably most convenient to keep everyone at whatever they have been doing before. But when the process of equalisation of costs and prices is begun, it will be necessary to draft labour from the contracting to the expanding occupations. A beginning could be made by asking for volunteers for removal to other works, and if anyone wishes to leave when contraction is needed he could be given his choice among the industries which are to be expanded.

There would still be little correlation between what people want to do and what the Ministry requires to be done, so that an adjustment will have to be carried out: this must be done by altering the relative attractiveness of occupations, which may be done in several ways. The simplest appears to be that of varying the wage or income payment, and this will be the one discussed now.

In order to restrain lazy or restless persons from making continual changes, some penalty would need to be imposed on those who leave their occupations, probably one which was cumulative—small for the first change and rising rather steeply. Subject to these provisions, all workers should be allowed to make application to be moved to other industries or districts. Where these applications are in opposite directions, i.e. where two men want to make moves the effect of which is that they exchange posts, an immediate transfer could be made. There will remain surpluses on one

side and deficiencies on the other which can
be kept on lists, presumably in order of priority
of application. These must be met by changes
in the standard rate of payment, in order to
change the relative attractiveness of the occupations. Thus if all the butchers wish to leave
their jobs and to become vegetable gardeners,
the payments to butchers will be increased and
those to the vegetable gardeners decreased:
at the same time the cost accounting for this
type of labour will be altered proportionately.
As it is unlikely that the cost of a labourer
will be the same as the payment to him, since
all income receivers are probably sharing to
some extent in the surplus receipts which in
the cost accounts are attributed to the capital
and the natural resources, the adjustment must
be proportional. Suppose, for example, that
there are n butchers and m gardeners; that the
labour of each is reckoned at 15s. per day and
that the standard income is 20s. per day (or
10s. as it might be if the state is not distributing as much in incomes as the labourers are
producing, perhaps owing to the expense of a
war or a large construction scheme). If it is
decided to lower the gardeners' payments to
18s., then the butchers can be raised to 20s.
plus $2m/n$; the total payments will be the same
as before. From a cost point of view, gardeners

will be reckoned in future at 18/20ths of 15s., and butchers at $20 + 2m/n/20$ths of 15s.

This will have a threefold effect in the direction required. (1) More vegetables and less meat will be sold to the public because with the new cost figures the price of the first will be lowered and that of the second raised, and budgets revised to an extent depending on the elasticities of the demands for these goods. Thus after production has been adjusted there will be more jobs for gardeners and less for butchers. (2) Some butchers will now be prepared to remain in the trade which before they wished to leave. (3) Some gardeners who were previously contented will desire to go to other industries now that the gardening rate has fallen, and some workers in other industries will be attracted towards the butchering trade which they previously disliked. It is probable that comparatively small changes in payment will be sufficient to bring about the state of affairs desired, which is that there will be just enough people who want to go into the trades in question to satisfy the requirements of the Ministry. Reductions of payment especially are likely to change the attractiveness of an industry, though we should not underestimate the effect of increases: overtime rates and "dirt money" produce surprising changes in the estimate of a given job. In any case, it is clear that *some* level can be found which will bring the supply of workers into relation with the available posts; if an occupation is sufficiently disliked, the Ministry will be forced eventually to charge such prices that all the consumers of its products will be choked off.

It might appear that we are now paying too little to the gardeners who remain gardeners and too much to the butchers who were content to go on even when they were only receiving 20s. There is certainly an advantage to the butchers who enjoy butchering, similar to that enjoyed by men with tastes which are cheaply gratified: it is an economic advantage to get more pleasure from water than from any other drink. But it is impossible to make any allowances for this sort of thing, if only because there is nothing to prevent any man from saying that he wishes to change if he knows that there is a shortage of his own kind of labour. It is the marginal cases which are important from the economic point of view; if they are satisfied, the intra-marginal will be more than satisfied, though we do not know to what extent. Equality cannot overcome the differences in personal tastes to this extent, and no-one can grumble at a situation when it is always open to him to put himself in anyone else's if he pleases. I cannot grumble at the high price of caviare which I like and the low price of winkles, which I do not: for I *could* buy as many winkles as the man who likes them.

So far we have been assuming that men have equal capacities and are therefore able to occupy any post which they choose if they are prepared to accept the payment ruling there. This is obviously untrue, and could only be believed by those with no experience whatever. But the question of differential capacities brings us to a difficult region. If everyone be willing to do his or her best, irrespective of the return, then it is of no consequence to the payments made that abilities differ. For they can be placed into groups which are roughly similar in capacity and some sort of average used corresponding to the marginal product for the purpose of cost accounting. But though their labour is charged at different rates according to the scarcity of their degree of ability, there is no need to pay them differently.

If, as is more likely, the intelligent and the strong are reluctant to occupy the posts of responsibility and strain, is there any way of getting them there? Since freedom is being allowed in the choice of occupations, the Ministry is precluded from using methods of compulsion, and in any case a clever man can conceal his abilities if he wishes to do so; no-one ever found any difficulty in failing in an examination. The inefficient can be prevented from taking posts for which they are unfitted by rules as to qualification, but if there is a shortage of qualified applicants there is no remedy except to lower the qualifications or find an inducement which will persuade the able to apply. It will be a serious matter if there are men of ability who are unwilling to go to those posts where they are required, so that the whole standard for the more arduous posts is lowered.

When Marx wrote of undifferentiated human labour, he was using an over-simplified concept of productive power; he was aware of the differences between men in this respect, and gives rough directions for comparing them. But the stress in his writing falls on labour as such, and it is common among Socialists to indulge in a sort of glorification of the unskilled labourer. From the point of view of production, which will control the standard of living, this is an unfortunate error; skilled work, and particularly the work of direction, is much more important, owing to the multiplication of its results. A failure of co-ordination may throw a whole department out for a considerable period, whereas the shortcomings of an unskilled labourer mean only the loss of some portion of his own time. The captain's work may be no more dignified, from the ethical point of view, than that of the cabin-boy, but if they exchange places the worst the captain can do is to leave the floor unswept or the plates dirty, while the cabin-boy may put the ship on the rocks, crew, floor, plates and all. Even if higher payments are made to the more skilled grades of labour, and especially to the skilled brain workers, it is likely that the total production will be so much higher than it would have been if with equal payments these men had not been willing to exert themselves that the payments to the other grades of labour will be higher than would be possible with equality.

It is, of course, possible that the more able will be induced to exert themselves although they are not offered a higher standard of living as a reward. Some men feel that it is worth doing a thing efficiently irrespective of the results to themselves, and by a suitable system of education this spirit could be made more prevalent. It is also possible to substitute inexpensive inducements in some cases: by the creation of orders of merit and so on. In Russia there is a system of special holidays, special rations, black lists, honour lists, statues of workers, and other devices for distinguishing those who give special services. Again, positions of power and responsibility have an appeal in themselves for some people, and it might be argued that only those who can fill them properly will be willing to accept them.

However, this is not invariably the case, and we are now considering those who will have to carry out tasks which, though responsible, will have a certain monotony about them. It is with creative and original work that men are most likely to do their best irrespective of monetary reward, and to some extent these men work because they expect the appreciation of those engaged in similar work. The giving of distinctions of the kind to which we have referred is more suitable for distinguishing the best of a class than for spurring on the whole class together. Privileges of any kind are much the same as differential money payments, and it is the opinion of the writer that these will have to be adopted until it can be shown that the social motive can be made effective by a changed education and environment. To some extent, the making of differential payments for special abilities is similar to the paying of different amounts according to the attractiveness or otherwise of the work, a principle which we have argued is in accordance with the

principle of equality, though the analogy is not
strictly applicable.

It is certainly true that in Russia the wage
system has become rather complicated in spite
of the original attempt to make payments more
or less equal; skilled workers get more than unskilled, piece-work has been adopted, and the
clerical classes are gradually raising their own
standards against that of the manual workers,
who were at first predominant. The example
of Russia has not been quoted very often in
this work because it does not appear to the
writer that the Russian planning offices have
followed rational principles in their economic
arrangements.[1] But in this case their experience is valuable as showing the difficulties in
the way of combining production with the
principle of equal incomes.

If this is admitted, and it is decided to pay
differential rates, the problem becomes much
the same as that of getting supplies of labour
to the unpleasant jobs: it is now to get supplies
of efficient labour. In the capitalist state the
worker tends to receive the value of the marginal product of the class of which he forms a
part, or his own specific product if he is the
only member of his class, and this can be com-

[1] See, e.g., Hoover, *The Economic Life of Soviet Russia*:
also the Appendix to this book.

puted; this would be the rent attributed to him from a comparison of output when he is working and when the next available substitute is taking his place, when he will get the market rate of the substitute plus the extra product. This method will give the upper limit to the amount which it will be worth paying him under Socialism. The lowest amount which should be paid is, of course, the average payment to all workers, subject to their being satisfactory to their foremen or managers. Among the less skilled grades of workers, the work done is similar for numbers of men and it is easy to say from an inspection whether the men are satisfactory or not.

The problem is therefore to find the level of wages for skilled and responsible posts which will make the holders do their best, and this can only be found by trial and error. It is certain that some of them will do their best for social reasons, so that there will be data for an estimate of what is to be expected from everyone; the payments offered can then be increased gradually until there is a satisfactory supply of labour which comes up to this standard. The amount necessary to persuade those with the necessary qualifications to offer themselves for the positions cannot be decided in advance, but it is probable that there will not need to be such differences in payments as correspond to the differences in productivity. For when most of the community are getting more or less the same amounts, comparatively small differences in income will be attractive. The experience of companies and of the public service shows us that if the men in responsible positions are getting enough to mark them off from their subordinates, they will feel some duty to perform their functions conscientiously and will find their work interesting for its own sake.[1]

The Russians have introduced piece-work rates in some of the lower grades of labour. It is the impression of the writer that these are generally unpopular among workers, and this is in itself an objection to them if the feeling should persist. It is necessary, however, that there should be some means of keeping up the standard of performance among workers, and this may have to be considered. It is not that the ordinary worker wishes to go slow or to scamp his work: there are few things so unsatisfactory as to have nothing or something obviously useless to do. But it seems to be true that there will always be some workers who take advantage of any relaxation of discipline

[1] Mr. R. F. Harrod has an interesting note on the whole subject in the *Economic Journal*, March 1936.

to relax their own efforts; and this has a most demoralising effect on the others, who feel a sense of injustice at finding no difference between themselves and those whom they know to be inefficient. In the interests of equality as well as of production, then, some standards must be kept. This brings us to the important question of the conditions of work and the position of the managers.

At one time it was the aim of workers' organisations to secure the control of industries for those who work in them: this was sought, for example, by the I.W.W. and by syndicalists and guild Socialists. It is doubtful whether this view is so popular as it was among the leaders of the Labour movement, and the economic difficulties of the position are well known; with any real workers' control, the interests of the industry and of the community are almost certain to diverge. The Ministry of Production, which is responsible for the economic arrangements, must not be hindered in its actions by pressure from particular classes of workers. On the other hand, one of the conditions of life which it is hoped to improve in a Socialist state is the position of the workers. It would probably be considered worth some sacrifice in the volume of production if the workers made a gain in the atmosphere in which they passed the working day, if these should turn out to be necessary alternatives.

There is no real opposition of interests between the Ministry aiming at the adjustment of production and the workers desiring an improvement in their psychological conditions. For the Ministry is concerned in this respect with the *relative* quantities produced, and this has little to do with the conditions of employment: it would only be material if the return to the workers depended on the results of each branch of production. But there might well be an opposition between the Ministry and the workers from the point of view of the *absolute* quantities produced, as there is certainly a connection between conditions of work and output.

This is a difficult matter to discuss and would need the careful consideration of those with a long experience of labour conditions from the sides both of the worker and of the manager. From the industrial experience of the writer, and from discussions with working men, I am of the opinion that security is most important to the average man and that he places next freedom from the exercise of arbitrary authority and from regulations which appear to be unnecessary in the situation. It is important to everyone to dismiss a man who endangers the lives of others or damages the capital equipment of the community; it is intolerable to dismiss him because he objects to the way he is spoken to if the manager is in a bad temper or has a dictatorial disposition.

This matter is only relevant from the aspect of economic arrangements because of the importance of the position of the managers, who will be responsible for the volume of production, and who must be given sufficient authority both to induce them to take the responsible posts and to allow them to carry out their duties efficiently. We have already considered the method by which their remuneration will be adjusted in order to get a satisfactory supply of such men, and it will be remembered that those who get the best results will be asked to expand their production from the surpluses of their costs over the receipts from the sale of their products. Probably payments to them which increased with the quantity of resources which they controlled would be found advantageous.

The workers will have security of employment, since there is no reason why there should be any unemployment except of the incapable or unwilling. They cannot be allowed to elect their managers, since the qualifications of the latter will be judged on their technical ability and on their success in keeping down costs.

And the managers must have the right to determine the methods to be followed and the distribution of labour to the various jobs, subject to the right of the workers to change their positions in the way already explained. But in order to secure the workers from arbitrary action, some form of elected works committee might be associated with the managers in all questions of discipline, with a right of appeal to officials of the Ministry, both in particular cases and against particular managers.

If the relations between workers and managers are always strained, production will be seriously impaired, and if this is likely, it is a reason for expecting the production of a Socialist economy to be low. There is therefore a responsibility on advocates of Socialism, if it should ever be put into practice, to attempt to produce as amicable relations as possible. Fortunately loyalty and common sense are not confined to any particular section of the community; there is no reason to suppose that the works committees, or whatever body is associated with the managers, will be invariably difficult.

We see, therefore, that there is likely to be a wage system and difference of payment according to the skill of the worker and to the general opinion as to the attractiveness or otherwise of

165

the work. As has been mentioned, it is unlikely that the differences will be so great as in a competitive society (differences in wages, that is; for there should be no income differences due to the uneven distribution of property). The higher levels of wages usually contain an element of surplus; they are rents which must be charged in costs, but, like true rents, are not necessary to call forth the supply of labour in question. In addition, there should be a greater mobility of labour, so that the higher levels of wages should not be due to any element of scarcity because of social reasons. In the capitalist world, wages differ because of differences in social advantages and because of the difficulty of movement between groups. Trade unions resist attempts to level the payments to labour, and employers are reluctant to annoy their men by taking advantage of cheap labour elsewhere to force wage-cuts.

In a Socialist state the obstacles of a social character should be small. Individuals in powerful positions may be able to do something for their relatives, but it is unlikely that there will be any privileged system of education or upbringing: in general, we should expect all children to go through the same educational mechanism. Trade unions, if they persist, may be a difficulty; if it were necessary to reduce

166

the wages of an industry in order to make it
less popular, the union in question might put
obstacles in the way. Such action would be
anti-social; the matter should be considered
by the men responsible for the policy of the
Socialist state.

Mention of education suggests that the needs
of the productive mechanism might be studied
in determining the educational system. It will
be a clear gain if the children are prepared to
work for the community, and only when this
is generally true will it be possible to have
substantial equality of incomes, assuming that
this is considered desirable. In *The First Men
in the Moon* Mr. H. G. Wells describes a society
in which the individuals were adapted from
their birth to the function which they were
going to carry out in the productive mechanism; this is something like Mr. Aldous Huxley's
Brave New World, in which the citizens were
adapted to want what they were going to get.
However, it seems more in keeping with ordinary concepts to train the children in some
general way, so that they will be citizens rather
than workers or consumers. Nevertheless some
special training will be required, and it should
be possible to decide at what stage each class
of worker should either leave school or go on
to vocational training. Many young men have

no idea as to what they want to do, and since the aim of the Ministry is to get labour at as nearly equal rates as possible, it will be an advantage to encourage those with no opinions to enter the occupations in which there was a shortage of labour.

In some occupations, such as the public services, which are financed by allocations from the Ministry instead of from the purchases of the consumers, it will not be possible to calculate the marginal product of labour. But once the total expenditure has been decided, the department concerned will only have to compete with other branches of industry in order to get the grade of labour required: the decision as to this should be left to the department, which is in the best position to know; e.g. if the War Office get £1000, they can get 5 good soldiers or 10 mediocre ones and they must themselves calculate which course is likely to give better results.

It seems desirable that decisions as to wage policy in general should be in the hands of a few highly paid and determined officials of the Ministry. As in the case of judges, it is of little importance if they are paid too much, since there are few of them and correct decisions are essential. Otherwise it is likely that the clerical grades of labour, who would control the mechanism, would tend to raise their own rates. But no-one should be allowed any say as to what he is to get: the only option is as to whether a man will take a job or not at the rate ruling for it.

In the case of non-workers, the incomes must usually be decided as a matter of policy. It should be easy to decide what is necessary for the upkeep of children and for proper care of the sick. If, which will be here assumed to be the case, there is no private saving, the aged and infirm should receive enough to make sure that they will not try to hoard large sums for their old age. There should be no unemployed, except the workers in transition from one occupation to another; and if there is some restriction against continual voluntary transfers, there should be full wages during such as take place owing to the desire of the Ministry to move labour from place to place. In the case of those who will not work, it appears that they will gradually drift to the lowest category of workers. If they are there considered unsatisfactory by the foremen or managers, they may be brought before a medical board. If this board decides that they are unfit to work, they can be placed in institutions if the cause is mental, or treated as any other case of illness if the cause is physical. But if there does not seem to be any reason of this kind, it will presumably be necessary to take some disciplinary measures, such as placing them in a labour camp or expelling them from the state. In a labour camp there may be some unpleasant work of social utility, and the men be kept on rations if they work to an adequate extent. But when the state offers work or maintenance, it should be in the position to say that if there is no work there will be no maintenance. "He who does not work, neither shall he eat."

CHAPTER X

MONEY

THE purpose of money is to facilitate the exchange of goods and to enable the accounts to be kept in terms of a common unit. Absolute prices are of no importance; only relative prices matter and *any* price-level is as good as any other. Hence *any* quantity of money will be satisfactory. It is necessary that it should be readily acceptable, since any doubt about it impairs its efficiency: in practice this means that it should be difficult to counterfeit and that the quantity should not be changed fast enough to lead to suspicions about the future of the price-level. Subject to the condition against forgery, the cheaper the material of the money the better: the modern forms of paper notes and metal tokens are perfectly satisfactory. It is hardly necessary to remark that no metallic backing is required; it is expensive and a positive embarrassment to a properly managed currency. The mismanagement of the currency by a Socialist state, though possible, would be extremely stupid and

171

a sign of weakness: anything which might be achieved thus could be much better done in other ways.

The Ministry, having decided on the prices and quantities of goods to be placed on the market in a unit period, must manufacture enough money to enable the total to be bought, and distribute it in the form of incomes; and must proceed to distribute this amount in every period, irrespective of the receipts. Any alterations made will be in the prices, which go up or down in the manner already explained, so that the prices which just clear the market are discovered. If there is no hoarding, the receipts per period of time must equal the payments. We shall discuss the question of hoarding shortly: let us first consider the case when there is none.

The great advantage of the Socialist state over the capitalist one is that the former does not have to meet its costs from its receipts, because its costs are only accounting concepts. This certainly removes the automatic check of the bankruptcy court, but it means that there need be no dislocation of production because of monetary causes. It is possible to short-circuit the monetary flow, paying the receipts from the consumers immediately back to them again, and thus giving a constant monetary

172

demand: relative prices become approximately correct indications of consumers' preferences.

But the prices of the goods are to be used in imputing the costs to the factors of production and it becomes necessary to consider the flow of prices backwards. If the short-circuiting takes place, the flow will not be a monetary one, but the calculations will be made in terms of the money, and important theoretical questions arise. In a capitalist society, much of the work of money consists in serving as the medium of payment from industry to industry: as the goods flow forward from the raw material through all their processes to the final stage in the hands of the consumers, the money flows backward; and only that part which is paid to the owners of the factors of production engaged in each particular stage becomes income available for the purchase of final goods at that stage.

Should the Socialist state do this also, paying the receipts from each stage to the managers of that stage and allowing them to buy for themselves the factors and semi-finished goods which they require? If this is done, there must be a complicated system of checks and of subsidies to the general income fund from the successful industries, or otherwise the advantages to be derived from the common ownership of the productive mechanism will be lost.

And in addition there will be monetary difficulties connected with the expansion and contraction of industry. It appears to the writer,
therefore, that all intermediate processes should
be costed in books without any actual money
passing. There will thus be the current money
used for paying incomes and for buying goods,
and the account money which is used for costing the processes, and which, like credit in a
capitalist state, is represented only by figures
in books. But since the accounts come from the
prices, the units will be the same.

The Ministry will then inform the productive enterprises of the figures at which they
are to reckon their resources, and they in turn
will supply figures of output and of marginal
costs where these can be reckoned. Average
costs are of course total costs divided by output. Since all units except the very small ones
discussed in Chapter VIII, are to keep books,
there is no extra trouble in using book figures
instead of actual money.

Let us now consider the relation between the
current money and the money of account, and
whether there is likely to be any reaction
between them which will interfere with the
calculations of the Ministry. This could take
place either if there were any chance of mixing
them up, or if the quantities used were not

appropriate to one another. But it is possible to avoid either of these things happening. If the accounts of transactions are all kept on paper and the payments all made in tangible money, they will not be confused so long as there is no way of turning the one into the other. The productive units will be credited with the proceeds of the sales, but the actual proceeds will go into whatever agencies make the payments. The productive units will be debited with their costs, including that of material which they purchase: if the plan of allowing them to expand from their surpluses is adopted, these will be earmarked and reduced as new capital is bought; but there will be no cash payments to make, for these are only made to the receivers of income and the spending departments, and they are paid by the agencies which receive the cash payments.

The two kinds of money could then only react on one another if rates of expansion, contraction, or change indicated by the one did not correspond to the rates indicated by the other; and especially if the funds to the credit of the various industries were generally positive, indicating the need for general expansion, so that resources were diverted from the making of consumers' goods to the making of capital goods. Now it has already been asserted

175

that the Ministry will have to decide in an arbitrary manner as to the rate of saving, and that it will do this by fixing the size of the industries producing capital goods. For new saving can only materialise to the extent of the capacity of these industries over the requirements of industry generally for depreciation. Any general tendency to expansion or contraction will be marked by a tendency towards activity or inactivity in these (the capital goods) industries, which will be met by a change in the rate of interest; while if it is attempted to expand with additional labour, the whole index of labour will be raised and its constituent parts accordingly. This increase in costs will in itself raise the price of new capital and check expansion. So long as the Ministry steadfastly refuses to alter the amount of activity in the capital-good industries, it can come to no harm from monetary miscalculations and these will automatically tend to correct themselves.

The Ministry will thus be in a strong position. It has only to adjust its costs so that the sum of these attributed in a unit period is equal to the sum of the prices received from the goods sold in the same period. The period chosen should be that found to be practically most convenient, and of course processes which take a longer or shorter interval must be reckoned at the appropriate fractions. It will be necessary to deduct the intermediate charges from stage to stage in the productive process, in order to avoid double reckoning. The two important indices, to recapitulate, are the state of employment of labour and of the capital-good industries, and the *relative* differences between costs and prices in the various industries.

Hence there should never be any unemployment. For the cause of this is the failure of capitalist industry to make profits generally: which must be due either to the factors of production forcing costs above prices, or to a failure of monetary demand for goods, thus bringing about a reduction in prices and thence of output and of employment. The Ministry itself determines the monetary demand for goods and fixes its own costs, and it can be indifferent to losses in general, which it will meet by altering its book figures of costs. It can also avoid any undesired transitional unemployment, for it can in effect subsidise industries which are making book losses until such time as it has prepared other occupations for the factors which will be displaced.

Hence the trade cycle should be non-existent. The difficulty of a capitalist economy comes from the fact that no-one can tell what people are going to do next with their money; for they can spend it, invest it, or hoard it, and no-one can do more than alter the relative attractiveness of these courses. But the uncertainty which attends the course of the trade cycle means that alterations in attractiveness will not necessarily bring about changes in the course of action of the individual.

Now in the Socialist state the individual is not allowed to invest his savings, since the Ministry controls the output of the capital-good industries. There is no financial circulation in Mr. Keynes' sense [1] of money used to finance transactions in titles to capital goods, for there are no such titles. All the movements of funds connected with capital transactions are movements of the book-keeping money and no-one can obtain any of this: the Ministry has it all under its own control. The individual can only spend or hoard his money. Let us now abandon the assumption that there is no hoarding and consider its effect on the monetary mechanism.

If incomes are assured and the state looks after sickness, old age, and education, and if savings cannot be invested, the main reasons for making them are removed. But there will

[1] *Treatise on Money*, by J. M. Keynes.

still remain the possibility of the unexpected, for which it will be desired by most men to accumulate some reserve. And if the state allows the possession of consumption capital, such as houses and motor-cars (which it would be well advised to do, owing to the pleasure which they give), there will be saving for these which may introduce some irregularity into the rate of spending. While hoards are being made, the monetary demand for goods must fall off and also the receipts of the institution which collects the funds for the payment of incomes. In the same way, when the hoards are spent, the monetary demand for goods increases and with it the receipts of the income-paying institution. On the principle of choosing prices which clear the market, this will lead to fluctuations in the price-level, and if production is adapted to this there will be changes in the levels of costs which will be inconvenient and may cause losses through adjustments which will not be permanent.

There is no difficulty about maintaining the level of incomes, since this can be done by manufacturing or destroying money to the requisite amount. This will avoid any cumulative tendency, and in itself should help to stabilise expenditure; that is, those who save should do so at a constant rate and the sums accumulated for buying houses, etc., should also reappear regularly. But the existence of hoards which may suddenly reappear remains an inconvenience and it would be advisable to have some control over them.

This might be done by setting up a state savings bank and perhaps paying a small rate of interest. In order to persuade the community to deposit their savings there, this bank must be ready to pay out deposits at all times without question; and no political use should be made of the knowledge gained as to the savings of individuals, except perhaps after their death, since it would be contrary to state policy to allow large sums to be accumulated through inheritance. If by these means the community were induced to make most of their hoards through the bank, the Ministry would know where they were and would have a check on its estimates of hoards, which are obtained of course from the difference between incomes and the receipts from sales.

It must now be decided what course is to be pursued with the voluntary savings: not the money, which can be accumulated, but the goods which are not bought because of the failure to spend all the incomes. To the extent that new saving is taking place, incomes are paid to the labourers producing capital goods, and so there are less consumable goods for others. The abstention from consumption by those who are doing voluntary saving will compensate to some extent for the saving forced upon everyone by the Ministry turning some of its resources to the production of capital goods; and this seems to be the best course to pursue. Any interest which may be paid to depositors in the savings banks will be some compensation to them, though we shall argue below that it is necessary on the whole for the Ministry to decide on the amount of saving. The only complication will occur if the depositors draw out all their savings and spend them at once (and the hoarders spend any hoards not deposited). If this happens, the price-level will be forced up for a time and those who possess savings will obtain some goods, though not so many as they have foregone, instead of the ones they might have bought if they had spent all their incomes at an even rate. The remainder of the community will suffer a reduction in their standard of living owing to the rise in prices. However, as soon as the savings are spent the price-level will return to normal again and the temporary inconvenience appears to be inevitable. If the Ministry has been successful in its other undertakings, this contingency appears to be an unlikely one and not worth the steps which would be required if it were resolved to avoid it altogether—these would be in the form of some hindrance to saving and would be difficult to enforce.

It may be seen therefore that with a strong policy there is no need for any monetary difficulties. The literature of economics on the subject of money is enormous, and the whole matter little understood. It seems proper to give some explanation of the very short treatment given here, since it is on the face of it most unlikely that anyone could treat so complex a subject adequately in a few pages. In a capitalist economy, which depends on the decisions of individuals for its motive powers, no-one is in a position to obtain a comprehensive view of what is being done with money; and the subject has to be treated deductively, arguing from what men ought to do when placed in certain situations. But what they do do is hardly known, because they act from a variety of motives, and especially because they are in a state of ignorance. There is therefore the possibility of a good deal of difference of opinion about the hypotheses upon which theories should be constructed: it is no wonder that the theories themselves differ. And since we cannot observe what is going on in men's minds, the inductive verification of the theories is always so imperfect that it is still possible for reasonable men to hold widely differing views.

But we have argued that in the Socialist state the position will be very much simplified; for the individual has his range of options narrowed considerably, and there are reasons for supposing that the main thing he will do with his money is to spend it. If the Ministry is indeed successful in eliminating cyclical movements of prices and of employment, the main reasons for irregularity in consumer's outlay are removed. And when we leave the outlay of the consumer, and enter the region of investment and of financial transactions, the individual is eliminated altogether: all the money here is controlled by a central undertaking, and there seems to be no reason why it should not know what it is doing. But if the courses to be followed are so simple, then the corresponding monetary theory will be simple. The Socialist state should have no monetary difficulties because it has removed from individuals the power of taking monetary decisions.

CHAPTER XI

THE PROBLEMS OF CHANGE

THE analysis in the abstract of problems of change, development, and progress is always unsatisfactory owing to the arbitrary nature of the assumptions upon which what we have called rational decisions are founded. The only changes which appear to be unequivocally beneficial are the substitution of cheaper for more expensive methods of production, and the closer adaptation of the quantities produced to those which will sell the goods at prices which measure the true scarcity of resources: we have already considered the mechanism by which these changes or rather adjustments can be made. In this chapter some consideration will be given to changes in those quantities which we have previously assumed to be known.

The question of foreign trade will be considered in the succeeding chapter, and inferentially the changes which follow from changes in external circumstances. Omitting these, changes may be classified as follows:

Changes in the tastes or preferences of consumers.

Changes in the methods of production.

Changes in the quantities of available resources.

In the last class are to be included changes in the numbers of the population; changes in the relative attractiveness of different kinds of work, and of work and leisure; changes in the amount of capital goods; and changes in the natural resources.

CHANGES IN CONSUMERS' PREFERENCES.— If these occur spontaneously, they present no difficulty, since they will be reflected in changes in the amounts of the finished goods which the community demand from the retail outlets. This will be followed by changes in price and the emergence of differences between prices and costs, and later by the transfer of resources: the process which we have described already as being required after erroneous calculations will serve for adjustments after changes in demand which make the previously correct calculations erroneous. But it is somewhat doubtful whether there will be any significant changes of this kind, for consumers in general do not change their tastes much: even in the case of women's clothing we may suspect that dressmakers are more active in changing

185

fashion than are those who wear the dresses. In the Socialist state it would be possible to allow all changes in fashions to originate with the consumers, who would be compelled to make their own dresses, thus altering the demand for material: the ready-made garments could then be altered in form when the change in taste has been established.[1]

In a capitalist state the principal agents in producing changes in demand are the entrepreneurs in their restless search for profits and a temporary respite from competition. Their agents are continually at work, persuading the consumers that they have wants hitherto unsuspected, or that their existing wants can be satisfied more completely by purchasing commodities different from those which they are actually purchasing. This is done partly by the various devices of advertising and selling, and partly by the continual invention of new com-

---

[1] My wife informs me that a valuable service is rendered by professional dressmakers to women who lack taste or skill in making their own clothes, and that there would be a loss of satisfaction and of specialisation if this class of workers were done away with. On the other hand, private establishments would presumably continue to make spontaneous changes in fashion if they were permitted. Possibly all the large retail outlets, which would be state-controlled, could have dressmaking departments. But there would need to be some control over them to prevent them competing through innovations in order to show that they were efficient and should be expanded.

modities, not previously demanded in at any rate this specific form because they did not exist.

It is sometimes possible to assert with a high degree of probability that a particular innovation has satisfied a want more fully than the good which has been displaced. Few will deny that a gas-stove is in general more convenient for the purpose of cooking than one fired with wood; or that a typewriter is usually a relief to those who have to read the communications of others. It is unlikely that this is always the case with inventions, and it is certainly not the case with all products which owe their success to advertising. The advocates of private enterprise may assert that whatever is a commercial success is best: the economist can only say that whatever is a commercial success is likely to persist. But the Socialist state by its fundamental tenet (no private property in the means of production) has abolished the profit-seeking entrepreneur and cannot avoid the task of making up its mind as to what it means by best.

We have already supposed that competitive advertising will be abolished: there is already a mechanism for finding the optimum size of the productive unit, and it cannot therefore be argued that such advertising will give economies

THE ECONOMIC SYSTEM IN A SOCIALIST STATE

in production which will more than save the resources devoted to it.[1] Any advertising which remains will therefore be informative, designed to ensure that the public is aware of what is available (this might well include statements about relative quality if it is possible to make them objective); or else to break down opinions which are thought to be prejudicial to the welfare of the community (*e.g.* against the use of soap or in favour of private enterprise). For this purpose a department of propaganda would be sufficient, organised on the principles of all unitary services; with a block vote and a specific aim to be reached as adequately as is compatible with the funds available. But it is inconceivable that this department would waste its energies in attempting to persuade the consumers of the truth of contrary propositions at the same time, such as that both A and B are the only possible cigarettes for the intelligent man.

The state therefore must do for the consumers whatever it considers necessary in the way of placing before them opportunities for changing their purchases. It must set up organisations which are charged with the duty of

[1] This is the usual defence of such advertising when it is thought necessary to defend it. It is doubtful whether it is valid when advertising has become general.

experiment and adaptation, and lay down limits both of expenditure and of policy within which these must function. We may classify the types of change as follows:

> Scientific or pure research.
> Invention and applied research.
> Improvement in method.
> Artistic or aesthetic change.

Scientific research, the pursuit of truth, is a good in itself for most societies, but is clearly one which must be paid for collectively, since the endowments by means of which it is financed in capitalist societies will no longer exist. The allocation of resources or funds for this purpose is one of the decisions to be made when the allocations for Government services are made, and as in all such cases, the organisation must be left to those considered most competent to carry it out. It is in the interests of everyone that those with the capacity for original research should be given a free hand; and pure research, having no commercial motive, cannot *in itself* lead to any changes in the economic structure.

Applied research is the application of scientific methods to specific problems. The experience of private firms, of institutes financed by industries as a whole, and of Government departments, indicates a satisfactory method for approaching such problems: for example, the treatment of refractory ores, the prevention or cure of diseases of living organisms, the discovery of substitutes for expensive materials, or those of which there is ground for fearing an eventual shortage of supply. In such cases it is generally obvious that a certain type of discovery will cause a marked economy, and it is possible to make a reasonable estimate of the probable cost of the research. The research may be unsuccessful, and in any case the economies will depend on the exact form of a discovery not yet made; but experience is a guide to the chances of success of applied research *taken as a whole*. From this we can arrive at an upper limit of justifiable cost, into the calculation of which the rate of interest will of course enter.

As the function of uncertainty bearing is one of great importance, and the question of whether it can be performed by a Socialist state is a controversial one, the last paragraph may be illustrated by a practical example. Anyone acquainted with the history of a particular industry will be able to supply others. The prickly pear plant in Australia, introduced as an ornamental shrub, spread with such rapidity as to constitute a menace to the great pastoral areas of the Eastern states.

In the twentieth century it was possible to calculate the area already covered and the annual rate of extension. The value of the land could be estimated by comparison with similar areas not yet affected, making allowances for the changed scarcities of complementary factors which would result from an increased area of land. Thus it was possible to calculate that Australia was losing so much every year from the existence of this plant.

From this it was possible to make calculations as to the maximum amounts which it would pay to spend on research on the assumption that in a given period a method of dealing with the pest would be discovered at an assumed cost per acre. It was not known either when, if ever, the remedy would be found, or what the cost of its application would be. But in the light of the experience of applied biology it was possible to take the best available advice as to probability and from this to decide whether the expense was justified: the state could then take the function of uncertainty bearing. The Governments which financed the research did not make these accurate calculations, as it was clear in this case that the results would outweigh the probable expenditure if any remedy were found at all. But if there had been any doubt, they could have made balancing estimates in this way. The same course is followed by firms when it is thought that the gains can be secured to those who make the discovery; and there is no reason why this course should not be pursued satisfactorily by a Socialist state.

The second kind of uncertainty is less amenable to calculation. As contrasted with the solution of problems already admitted to exist, we have the inventions which are not foreseen, at any rate by the leaders of the industry, which are to some extent the result of a happy accident: the sight of the saw with cotton fibres adhering, protruding through the wall; the desire of the child operating the steam-valves to play in peace. In most cases of spontaneous invention, the inventor needs to have faith in his idea and to have the possibility of obtaining resources while he works upon it. The captains of industry do not usually see the possibilities of entirely new ideas when these are in embryo, nor are these in a form in which they will commend themselves to the public. Only when the invention is established is there any reward from it, and if this does not happen the brunt of the loss is borne in the capitalist economy by those who believed in ultimate success.

Now in these cases there does not seem to

be any criterion by which the Socialist state can decide the amount of resources which it is proper to spend: so that they cannot rationally create a profession of inventors. On the other hand, if these matters are left to the chance on which they depend the path of the innovator will be even harder than it is in the capitalist state. In the interests of economy it is necessary to discourage the cranks; but it is probable that the leaders of industry will consider that all innovators are cranks. In the capitalist state the inventor is free to devote any resources which he inherits, or can earn or can wheedle from patrons, to his researches. In a Socialist state he will get nothing which he does not earn and he may find himself in a labour camp if he neglects his work. The progress of spontaneous invention may well be slowed unless care is devoted to preserving a receptive frame of mind in the higher officials. But if they are too receptive there may be dissipation of the national resources in grandiose projections doomed to failure. It is difficult to follow a middle course when no-one knows where the middle is: the Socialist state will have no certainty, nor can any other form of organisation give it.

Improvements in method hardly need separate consideration; where they are not the result of applied research they will come from the encouragement given to the managers of undertakings to reduce their costs, and we have already considered a mechanism by which they can be passed on.

With regard to the restless changes of fabric, pattern, and style which mark the retail market in a competitive economy, it is easy to make changes for the sake of change if this is considered desirable. We cannot attach a market value to variety which will have any ultimate meaning. But the state factories engaged in producing commodities which embody the achievements of the decorative arts can have departments of design; and they can impose any degree of change which they or the Ministry think expedient by offering employment to the appropriate number of young artists. The response of the consumer to these changes will give some indication as to which of them is popular; but it is difficult to form an opinion about the validity of any index designed to measure the desire of the public for variety.

Mention of the decorative arts suggests the consideration of the position of the arts generally, and of their commercial applications. It has been the custom of many societies to subsidise artistic creation of every kind, the scale of values adopted being obviously other than an economic one. Many people hope that the Socialist state will not be behind the court or the millionaire in this respect. The appropriation to be made and the method of distributing it are matters of policy.

The arts in general are related to economic questions in so far as the products of artists are demanded and purchased by the public in the form of books, pictures, etc., and of dramatic and musical entertainments. Entertainments, which require organisation, are an easy matter, and the Continental practice of organising state theatres and opera-houses shows that the state need find no difficulty in conducting such enterprises. Whatever subsidies are thought desirable can be given by providing the entertainments at less than cost or gratis: though rationing will be involved if anything but open air concerts be given free, and, as we have seen, there is a *prima facie* case against rationing.

On the other hand, books and pictures are produced by an essentially individual process and it is doubtful whether it would be wise to establish colonies of writers or blocks of studios. The state can provide facilities for those who wish to write or paint, so that they can place their works before the public. And if it can decide on an absolute standard, it can combine its policy of subsidising the deserving with its dislike of large private incomes by varying the outflow of incomes to artists and writers. It is in the position of a universal agent with a monopoly, who supports the promising young men and charges large commissions to the successful.

CHANGES IN THE QUANTITIES OF AVAILABLE RESOURCES.—If no wars of conquest are won or lost, the amount of the natural resources of any country is a fixed quantity; the alterations in potentialities which occur are due to changes in knowledge or changes in methods, and are comparable in their effects to changes towards a more economical use of any kind of resources. We have described the process by which the appropriate margin for any set of conditions may be found, and the process of change to suit different circumstances.

The numbers of the population are obviously likely to change. And except in pioneering societies which enjoy extensive resources and a knowledge of productive methods derived from more densely settled areas, an increase in population unaccompanied by a proportionate increase in capital is likely to reduce the average output per head. This follows directly from the shape of the cost curves for productive units, which are rising at the point of equilibrium. It is unlikely that the increased demands of a larger population will allow of the rearrangement of the existing capital so that economies from larger plants could be secured; in any case the rearrangement of capital goods is a slow process. The question of changes in numbers cannot therefore be studied without considering the policy to be pursued with regard to capital accumulation. If we assume that there will be at least enough saving to keep the average capital per head constant, then the optimum population can be considered. The maximum output per head with a given average capital is obtainable when the advantages from increasing division of labour just offset the disadvantages arising from the recession of the various margins marking the limit of profitable exploitation of the natural resources. As the exact point at which this balance is reached cannot be found, the most for which any society can hope is that it will be able to avoid obvious pressure of population on natural resources. It is a matter of great difficulty to control the size of the population without interfering with the private lives of the individual members of society: the end is only one of many desirable ones, and the means must be balanced against it if these involve conflict with some other end. It might be found expedient to use some sort of propaganda to influence changes in numbers in the direction desired. Otherwise gradual changes in population do not appear to cause any particular difficulties of adjustment. The capital which is being accumulated for the extra people takes the form of additional houses, schools, work-places, etc.; to the extent that an increase in the use of land is necessary, the average output will show a falling tendency. But it is likely that for moderate increases of numbers which seem more likely than large ones in modern societies using contraceptives,[1] improvements in methods will outrun the decreases in output which occur because of diminishing returns. It is easy to find out how the composition of the population is likely to change over quite long periods, so that steps can be taken to expand capital in the appropriate direction. Large migrations would create awkward problems, but these can be discouraged to any extent desired by lowering the whole level of payments to the workers in any area which shows unwelcome signs of expanding population. Indeed this step will be taken automatically as soon as workers begin to apply in

[1] It is possible that decreases will be more usual than increases. See, for example, Dr. Enid Charles, *Memorandum* for the Royal Economic Society, No. 55.

increasing numbers for employment in any particular district.

CHANGES IN CAPITAL.—The amount of savings in any year is completely under the control of the Ministry, and is expressed by the amount of resources devoted to the construction of capital goods. It has already been explained in our discussion of the monetary system that there should be no difficulty about preventing stocks from accumulating because the community wish to save some of their incomes; and since they are unable to have any effect on the volume of employment in constructional industries, capital accumulation is independent of individual decisions.

It has been suggested that there will be a loss to the community if this course is adopted, because some people suffer less from saving than others: when the Ministry decides on the amount to be saved it inflicts an equal reduction of income all round, instead of allowing the burden to be taken by those who will feel it least. The Ministry might establish a system by which those who felt inclined to reduce their consumption could make voluntary contributions towards national accumulation, but it is unlikely that it could obtain enough funds in this way to carry out the programmes it considered necessary. It would therefore be compelled to offer whatever interest was necessary to produce the required sums, which would result in a variety of complications in connection with the ownership of the bonds and the incomes arising from the interest payments on them.

It has also been suggested[1] that the Socialist state cannot find out the right rate of saving because it is not allowing the community to decide, through the rate of interest, upon how much future income is worth particular reductions in the present. In a competitive society it is open to every individual to restrict his present consumption as much as he pleases, and in return to obtain a larger consumption in future; and no doubt everyone is affected to some extent by the rate of interest when he considers the last unit which he will save or spend. Since the sum of individual decisions constitutes the whole decision, it may be argued that the amount saved at any time is the amount which the community thinks it is worth while to save. The root of the economic system is the individual balancing of alternatives, and if we try to allow this in the commodity market, we should also wish to secure it in respect of saving.

[1] See H. D. Dickinson, "Price Formation in a Socialist Community," *Economic Journal*, June 1933, p. 244.

It is extremely doubtful whether any such position is a tenable one. The amount of saving in actual capitalist societies depends on the actions of companies and of the Government at least as much as it does on individual decisions; and the slightest acquaintance with monetary theory shows us that the results of individual decisions are so much affected by reactions from the trade cycle that there is at any time little connection between what individuals are trying to do and what is actually happening. The Socialist state will at least be able to avoid the painful spectacle of seeing its savings being wasted while its constructional trades are idle owing to a fall in the price-level. However, even if we compare it with the frictionless state where there are no monetary complications, it is difficult to find any ground for preferring one or the other.

The aim of the state is the welfare of its citizens, and in the strictly capitalist state these must be supposed to benefit from its existence differently according to the differences in their incomes—not proportionately, but to the extent, whatever it is, that the total satisfaction obtainable increases with increase of income. In considering the optimum amount of saving, we must be supposed to be aiming at the best for the community. There are two

THE ECONOMIC SYSTEM IN A SOCIALIST STATE

difficulties: can we identify the sum of what each man thinks will be best for himself with what will be best for them all taken together? and since the community goes on although the present members of it die, can we assume that the sum of present actions will be best for the future generation as well as for the present one? If the present generation ask "What has posterity done for us?", in what sense can it be argued that it is acting for the best?

The difficulty is the same as that which is encountered when we try to compare various distributions of income: we do not know how to count the individuals, with the added complication of needing to count the minors and the unborn as well. Thus it is impossible to defend or to attack any particular position except on general or common-sense grounds. Most men would agree with Mr. Winston Churchill's words, "We are only life-tenants" of the capital equipment of the country, and would feel some moral obligation to hand it on in at least as good a condition as it was received. It seems to the writer that there is also some duty to increase the capital of the country, and this is stronger the more inadequate the present amount is. But the fact that it is necessary to use such words as "moral obligation" and "duty" shows that there is no question of accurate calculation and that we are dealing with decisions which not only may be, but ought to be, taken by the community as a whole, that is to say with political decisions. Thus the rate of interest will not have the function of securing the supply of capital, but only of rationing the actual supply among the various competing uses.

The supply, as we have said, is given by the size of the industries producing capital goods, and in particular the building and constructional trades and the machine-making industries. The first call on these will be the making good of depreciation of the existing stock of houses, factories, machines, means of transport, etc.; and any surplus capacity will be new saving, the use of resources which might have made consumption goods for making capital goods. We have already considered the mechanism by means of which the new capital will be allocated to industries, those showing the greatest difference between prices and costs being allowed to expand first. But there are a number of problems in this connection which will need consideration, especially after equilibrium has been reached so that all industries are just earning the current rate of interest and therefore are not required either to expand or to contract.

It is necessary to make a clear distinction between expenditure on income account and that on capital account. All existing capital except that which is to be allowed to depreciate to nothing must be kept intact, and for this purpose an estimate made of the annual depreciation; even if this is not made good in any particular year, the sum must be charged against the enterprise which is using the plant. Buildings and machines usually need minor annual repairs which can be done by members of the staff, and this expenditure will cause no difficulties as it is charged at once to the annual costs. But when the plant is worn out or obsolete, it must be replaced by purchases from the industries making capital goods. For this purpose it is usual in the capitalist economy to accumulate funds which are employed temporarily for other purposes, such as reducing the bank overdraft or increasing holdings of securities. There is a tendency owing to the influence of the trade cycle for enterprises to try to make replacements at the same time, but it is plainly desirable that they should come in rotation in order to keep the resources employed in the capital goods industries as small as possible for the work to be done, *i.e.* that there should be full employment of these resources.

In the Socialist state, two conditions are to be satisfied: the total paid in to the central obsolescence fund by all industries in any year should be spent in that year, and each concern should spend in the period of the lifetime of its equipment an amount equal to what it has paid in, accumulated at compound interest. Thus an order of preference must be constructed and adhered to, so as to give this even rotation. Some difficulties may be caused in the early stages, as there will be a tendency to crowd the work in the later years. The problem is like that of keeping a fleet up to date: if we start with all the ships new, either some must be scrapped before they are worn out, or some retained in service after they should have been replaced, or else the replacement cannot be even. But once a rotation has been established it will go on automatically. It is necessary to pay interest to the concerns in order to weight the scales correctly in favour of those which make their capital last longest, and this means that the capital-good industries will have to be subsidised from general funds, since the annual payments from the obsolescence allowances will be less than the value of work done for replacements. But it is proper that this subsidy should be paid, since during the period which originally elapses between the payment of the first depreciation allowance and the first work of replacement, the economic system is acquiring new capital which is made by the industries which will later be required to work for depreciation. The community has more capital than it otherwise would have had and its income is larger: it is from this extra income that the interest on the accumulating funds can be paid.

In the same way the Government departments, such as the fleet and the education service, must distinguish between repairs and new expenditure. It will be remembered that these receive block grants to spend in the way which they consider will give the best results. Part of the grants will be set aside in order to keep the equipment intact, and the procedure with regard to depreciation will be exactly the same as that which we have just discussed. But these departments must not be allowed to spend any of their grants on new construction, for this will both upset the scale of activity in the capital-good industries and also involve them in difficulties with the calls on their incomes later. How, then, can they expand themselves? In order to answer this question we must now consider the process of capital expansion as a whole.

In the period of transition from a position

which is out of equilibrium to one which is not, we have seen that there are many possible rates of movement. The industries which are not covering their costs decline while the others expand, but there is no criterion by which to decide on the amount of capital construction which will be warranted. If all the profits of the industries which should expand are turned back into the means of expansion, it is possible that the capital-good industries will be too large and that there will be dislocation when the position of equilibrium has been reached. For this reason it was suggested that the adjustment should be governed by the determination to keep the capital-producing industries at a fixed size. If it is decided to save more than before, the first requirement will be to expand these industries themselves.[1]

However it is decided, there must be some conscious decision as to how much to save above the requirements for depreciation; and the decision is a political one, into which such considerations as the foreign relations of the

---

[1] The Russians do not seem to have been so indifferent to economic considerations as has been suggested in their determination to expand their heavy industries, although it would have been more apparently profitable to expand the industries producing consumption goods. For an expansion of these industries is an essential prerequisite of almost any other expansion.

State, the educational facilities, and the temper of the inhabitants will enter, as well as considerations of the standard of living at the moment and the opportunities for increasing this by means of better equipment. Having made this decision, an order of preference will have to be constructed. If there is no problem such as that of defence, which must be set above all others, it seems reasonable to work first at bringing the existing industries into equilibrium, if this needs to be done faster than is allowed for by diverting the depreciation allowances. When this is achieved, then there are two guides. The Government departments have no profit-and-loss statements and cannot show by their books that they should be expanded: their place in the priority list must be decided on the same grounds as is their annual allocation, that is by considerations of social expediency in relation to the general economic position. The remaining departments, the productive ones, can show that they are earning the rate of interest on the capital that they use and can put forward prospective profits in order to claim their own places.

In the absence of such claims it will be necessary to lower the rate of interest or to reduce the amount saved and thus the size of the capital-good industries. But there are several sources which are likely to call for new capital, and which must be scrutinised with care. There are always undertakings such as railways and roads which will use a great deal and the yield of which it is difficult to work out accurately in advance. Small errors in the amount of depreciation allowed for are sufficient to vitiate the preliminary calculations, and it is likely that there will always be a number of expensive projects on the list to which recourse can be had if there is any shortage of outlets for savings. It will be necessary to have the priority list well ahead of time so that careful planning can be made for the use of displaced resources.

The effect of new inventions which will immediately make existing capital obsolete also needs consideration. Changes in technique, either discovered at home or copied from abroad, will change the priority lists, and some rule must be made about giving effect to them. The existence of old plants and machinery means that it will pay to work them as long as direct costs, labour, raw material, power, etc., are lower than total costs, including interest and depreciation with the new plant. If this condition is satisfied, it is only necessary to replace old machines with new as fast as the old ones wear out. The proper price for the goods is the total price in the new conditions and the cost of the new machines, etc., should be found whether sufficient sums have been accumulated or not. But if the new methods are cheaper than the direct costs of the old, then the replacement of the old capital will take a high place in the order of priority.

If it is necessary to reduce the rate of interest, it is clear that the relation between the cost of capital and its marginal productivity will be disturbed and there will be a general tendency to expand the use of capital everywhere; in particular in those occupations which use large amounts of it already. And it is no doubt hoped by the advocates of the form of society which we have been discussing that this will take place on a large scale and that, as a result, the length of the working day will be reduced. But it seems unlikely that there will be much need to search for outlets for savings, for there is likely always to be a number of projects of doubtful economic value but dear to the imaginations of the rulers of the state; and there is also a large outlet in the increase of consumption capital, such as houses and appliances for use in them, which will absorb great quantities for small reductions in the rate of interest.

Finally let us consider the question of the length of the working day and the attitude of the public towards income and leisure respectively. These should be treated as inversely related parts of the real income, at any rate until the working day has got so short that it is generally considered a pleasure to work. For most people, however, it seems probable that there will be the choice of working more and getting more goods or having more leisure with less to consume. And it must be decided to what extent the workers will be allowed to make this choice. From the point of view of consumption, the best arrangement would be to allow everyone to work as long as he pleased with an income to correspond, the income being so much per hour's work for all those who have to work at all, presumably everyone but the children, the old and the infirm: possibly also married women if the state takes the view that this is expedient. But owing to the necessities of production there will probably have to be a regular supply of labour: to obtain the economies which are possible with capital it is necessary to co-ordinate the workers, and this is difficult if they come and go as they please. There are many occupations in which this is not strictly necessary, and it will be advantageous to preserve any casual trades or

211

even handicrafts in order to give an outlet to those of the populace who dislike routine work, it being clear that the incomes will be kept down in such a way as to check an undue influx of labour to these occupations. (That is, workers here will not be paid in proportion to those elsewhere, with the only differences due to the differences of hours; but according to the principles enunciated in Chapter IX.)

This will give some scope for choosing the hours to be worked individually. But there does not seem to be any reason why the workers as a whole should not have some voice in the hours which they are to work, as long as the managers or directors are allowed to arrange the times of work so that they will know where they are when they are making their arrangements. Frequent changes of hours will upset all the plans of the Ministry, since they will cause changes in the quantities of goods to be produced, and hence their scarcities and prices; so that some independence in this respect must be sacrificed in the interests of efficiency of the whole system. But it should be possible to take the opinions of the workers from time to time about the length of the day and the period of holidays, and to make experiments gradually. If the workers in the Socialist state are anything like those of capitalist economies, it is likely that they will prefer general reductions of hours to reductions in some enterprises accompanied by income reductions there; and that they will prefer the reductions of hours to take place at a time when the efficiency of production is increasing so that the reduction comes instead of a reduction of the prices of goods. But as we cannot generalise about something which must be a matter of fact, all that is necessary is to point out that if experiments are made slowly it should be possible to allow the community as a whole to choose their working hours. Indeed it would be quite possible to have workers in the same occupations working for different times, one factory having an eight-hour day, another a six-hour day, and so on; though this would complicate somewhat the work of calculation to be done by the Ministry.

In all cases of change it must be remembered that changes are disturbing and usually cause losses during the period of adjustment. And for this reason it seems desirable to place some obstacles in the way of all changes so that they will not be embarked upon in a capricious spirit. When it is clear that they are wanted or necessary, they should be made with decision; but it would be well in every case to wait until those who want them are unmistakably prepared to sacrifice something in order to obtain them.

NOTE TO CHAPTER XI

Professor F. H. Knight has a paper in the Supplement to *The American Economic Review*, March 1936, on The Place of Marginal Economics in a Collectivist System. If I have understood him aright, Professor Knight takes the view that (1) the Socialist state will be developing so rapidly that a stationary analysis will be inapplicable; (2) where the decisions as to the direction of change are made by a central executive, no *economic* analysis of a dynamic nature can be applied either. Hence the proper attitude of the economist is to be silent. I feel very doubtful about (1) and have some doubts about (2).

CHAPTER XII

INTERNATIONAL TRADE

THE advantages of international trade are familiar to all students of Economics; production is increased by specialisation, and it is plain that geographical causes make it extremely difficult for some countries to produce certain products, such as tropical plants and minerals. Many books are devoted entirely to this subject and there is no disagreement about the underlying principles. In practice a number of difficulties of a frictional character occur, and in the attempt to ameliorate these and to obtain as much self-sufficiency as possible all countries impose obstacles of various kinds to the free exchange of goods between them. The Socialist state is in a fortunate position with regard to its own frictional forces, owing to its independence of short-run profits and losses; it will have to take account of the possibilities of friction elsewhere and will, of course, have to attach some weight to the dangers of external supplies if it expects them to be interrupted.

The general principle is that of comparative costs. If the ratio between the marginal costs of production of any two products in one country is different from the ratio of the marginal costs of the same two products in another country, then it will pay each country to exchange the goods in which it has the comparative advantage for that in which it has the comparative disadvantage. The goods which will be exchanged in conditions of equilibrium cannot be decided exactly from an original inspection of the comparative costs, owing to changes in the margin of production which will occur after trade has begun: the comparative costs being the marginal ones, a number of possible cost ratios exist. The exact goods and quantities to be exchanged will only be determined after introducing the second condition of equilibrium, referred to in the next paragraph. Equilibrium is reached when the ratio of the marginal costs has become the same, which occurs when the production takes place in conditions of increasing costs, through the extension of the margin of production of the commodity being given and the contraction of the margin of production of the commodity being received. In the extreme case, each country may abandon the production of one commodity entirely and get all its supplies from the other in return for the commodity on the production of which it now concentrates: this happens with such commodities as rubber and coffee, and also with certain metals. The rate of exchange of the commodities will be somewhere between the two rates previously existing, which must in each case have been equal to the marginal costs. (These propositions do not apply to the unusual case in which the commodities or either of them are produced in monopolistic conditions.) The exact position of the new rate of exchange will depend on the combined demands for each commodity and the supplies of each.

It is further necessary for equilibrium that the value of all the exports of a country, including the so-called invisible items, should equal the value of all the imports similarly increased. This condition is always satisfied by the inclusion of a balancing item of short-term indebtedness: over longer periods, in which it is unusual to accumulate short-term credit balances, either the rate of exchange, or the level of internal money costs, or the volume of unemployment, must be moved so that the external trade balances without the accumulation of short debts. It is these balancing movements which have introduced such complexities into the practice of international trade of recent years and led to the somewhat irrational structure which now exists in the world.

The Socialist state must therefore aim at securing the advantages which can be obtained from the difference between its comparative costs and those existing elsewhere, and it must also seek to balance its international transactions, in which we may include long-term borrowing and lending. It should first decide the question as to whether there are any key industries which are necessary to the economic structure or to the conduct of any wars in which it has reason to expect that it may be involved. It is generally admitted that it is prudent to maintain such industries although the products could be obtained with less expenditure of resources by producing other commodities and exporting them, the additional cost being an insurance premium. The importance to be attached to this factor will obviously depend on the likelihood of supplies being interrupted, whether by wars or by other circumstances which may alter the world supplies.

There is no difficulty about finding the internal marginal costs, since if the calculations already stated to be essential have been made, these will all be available. In most cases there will also be market prices existing in the

countries to which the Socialist state has
access, so that the comparison of costs can
be made at once. If Russian timber costs
2000 roubles a standard delivered at ports
and can be sold there to an English merchant
for £18, and if steel bars also cost 2000 roubles
to produce, but can be delivered from England
at £10 per ton, then it is clearly advantageous
for Russia to buy steel in England and obtain
the sterling required by exports of timber.
The sales of timber will probably depress the
world price, and the extension of production
in Russia should increase the cost of production there if it had previously been cut in the
most convenient forests; and it is possible that
the purchases of steel will raise the world
price. The steel should be charged to the enterprises which use it at its cost in terms of timber
cost, that is at Cost of timber per standard in
roubles × Sterling price of steel per ton/Sterling
price of timber per standard. If this rises to
2000 roubles it will then be worth maintaining
steel-works: otherwise the Russian demand for
steel should be satisfied by imports. It is clear
that if Russia produced its own steel before,
there should be enough resources released to
provide the additional timber: the price of
timber will rise and less of it be consumed, but
on the lines indicated in Chapter II it can be

shown that the loss of timber is more than compensated for by the increase of steel. It is unlikely that all the extra productivity will be taken out in steel; in most cases some of the freed resources will be available for other forms of production.

The process of calculation becomes more complex when there are a number of commodities, but it would be possible to carry it out on the lines indicated. The costs of all commodities produced at home would be compared with the prices obtainable abroad if they were sold there, and the prices which would have to be paid if they were bought there: these prices are not the same owing to transport costs and tariffs, if these exist, and will differ from country to country because of these circumstances, so that one part of the production exported may be sold at a higher price than is obtainable for the remainder. A list of products may be drawn up in order of advantage, those with the greatest comparative advantage at the top and those with the least at the bottom. All the foreign prices can be done in terms of one currency, using the current exchange rates to get cross rates where the transactions are to be carried out in a number of countries. It will then be possible to begin exporting the products at the head

220

of the list and importing those at the bottom. Import will cease when the local demand is satisfied at the prices calculated, as above explained, or when home production can be begun at this price: exports cease when the home cost has risen to the figure which makes comparative cost ratios equal. As the process continues, new commodities will be imported and new ones exported at the same time as the margin of production on the earlier ones extends: the marginal costs in equilibrium will all bear the same relationships as the world marginal costs. Finally, there will be no comparative advantage left. At every stage the trade will balance, since it is the receipts from exports which are used to pay for the imports.

If the Ministry is prepared to establish an exchange rate, this process can be done in a different manner which is also rather simpler. An arbitrary rate of exchange can be established for purposes of calculation, between the internal currency and the currencies of the world: again any of them, but preferably one which is widely used and fairly stable (such as sterling), will do, and cross rates calculated for the others from the world exchange quotations. The prices at home and abroad can then be compared directly through this rate; if it

THE ECONOMIC SYSTEM IN A SOCIALIST STATE

is 125 roubles to the pound sterling, then in our previous example a standard of timber can be produced for £16 and a ton of steel for the same amount. Now everything which can be produced more cheaply than the amount for which it will sell abroad can be exported, such as timber; and everything which can be bought abroad for less than it costs to make at home can be imported, such as steel: the goods sent abroad are produced on a larger scale until the falling prices received meet the rising marginal home costs. The goods imported are sold at world prices translated into home prices at the given exchange rate. It will then be found either that stocks of foreign currency are accumulating or that not enough of them can be obtained to purchase the imports. In each case the exchange rate must be moved: in the first upward (making imports cheaper and export receipts lower in terms of home currency) and in the second downwards. Finally, a rate would be found at which the supply of foreign currency will just balance the demand for it, and the disposition of imports and exports would be the same as if the process explained in the last paragraph had been followed. There are no differences between internal and external ratios of costs.

It would be possible to modify this pro-

cedure in order to exploit the monopoly of
external trade which is allowed by the unified
control of it. This involves calculations of the
effect on the world prices of the sales and purchases of the Socialist state, and is not worth
doing unless its share of the world trade in the
commodity under consideration is substantial.
In the case of exports, the world conditions of
supply and demand are estimated and thus a
demand schedule constructed for various quantities sold by the state. From this a marginal
revenue curve can be found, *i.e.* a curve showing the increment of receipts from selling an
additional quantity, allowing for the reduction
in price which would have to be made on the
previous sales. To gain the maximum advantage, the marginal revenue and not the price
should be made equal to the internal marginal
costs. In the same way, if the result of purchases abroad is to raise the price against the
buying country, the cost of an additional
amount is really its price plus the increase of
price on the amount previously bought: which
may be termed the marginal outlay.[1] The marginal outlay will then have to be made equal

[1] The terminology is somewhat loose. Additional sales or
purchases cannot affect *previous* transactions; but as the
trade will usually be continuous the calculations required
are of possible alternatives, each one of which if chosen
excludes all the others.

to the marginal costs of producing the goods exported to pay for them.

In these ways there would be the possibility of obtaining some advantage from the rest of the world: a procedure of doubtful expediency, and one which might lead to reprisals if the markets in which sales and purchases were to be made were at all restricted. If reprisals are made, the problem of the rate of exchange of goods becomes highly complex. It has been discussed by a number of writers on the subject of International Trade. There is a variety of positions all of which are of advantage to both parties, and the final one depends on the bargaining powers of each. But taking them as a whole, the most advantageous position is that which would be reached if no attempt were made on either side to control the course of events; and at any rate between Socialist states we may hope that this will be done.[1]

We must also consider briefly the non-merchandise transactions in which a Socialist country might engage. If the citizens are to be allowed out of the country and tourists are to

[1] When the Socialist state is dealing with countries which have tariffs against its own products, it may be necessary to consider whether it should not act as a monopolist. Possible situations of this sort are suggested by Edgeworth in his "Pure Theory of International Values", *Collected Papers*, Section IV.

be allowed to come in, there must be some rate of exchange: the obvious one to use is the rate being used by the foreign trade corporation, if the second of the above methods has been chosen. If the first is in use, some sort of index-number calculation of purchasing power parities may be made, so that a unit of home currency will buy the same sort of things in the same amounts as the amount of the foreign currency to be given for a unit of home currency will buy in the foreign country. It will not matter if the rate is not a very accurate one, as the market for this kind of transaction is restricted to tourists. If the tourist industry is considered a valuable one, it could be subject to the rules of a discriminating monopoly by adjusting the hotel charges for each type of traveller; or, special rates of exchange might be made in order to get the maximum revenue from the tourists as a whole. But there is little to be said for any of these attempts to exploit the foreigner.

The question of transport and especially of shipping is a simple one. If there are no political reasons on account of which it is considered necessary to develop a national merchant marine, then the principles of comparative cost show whether it is cheaper to do your own carrying or to have it done for you: usually it will be cheaper to do some of it, but there will be a balance one way or the other, which is treated as an import or export as the case may be. The country which is carrying for others needs to export less, and that which has its carrying done for it to export more, than appears to be necessary when this item is neglected.

Finally, we need to consider movements of capital and international payments of interest. As the late Professor Pierson pointed out in his essay on "The Problem of Value in the Socialist Community",[1] ". . . the general interest of mankind [demands] that only such capital be applied to international trade as cannot be more productively employed in other branches of earning". In order to carry on international trade, stocks will have to be accumulated and kept, and this represents an act of saving which, if turned to some other purpose, would have increased the capital and the volume of production there. Hence the cost of the imports for purposes of calculation will be increased by the interest on their cost between the time of paying for them and the time of using them; and the receipts from selling exports will be diminished by the interest on their value when

[1] Reprinted in *Collectivist Economic Planning*, edited by Professor von Hayek.

the true cost of producing and selling them is calculated. Now international trade in general is financed from the centres of the world's trade in which money is cheapest, according to the rule given by Professor Pierson. And it is clear that if the rate of interest which has emerged as a result of the pricing of the factors is higher than the rate at which money can be borrowed abroad, it will pay to have the international trade financed from there, so that capital will not need to be diverted from internal uses. This can be done by financing the trade by means of bills given to the sellers of the imports and received from the buyers of the exports, which can then be discounted in the cheapest centre. In order to be able to do this, all bills should be met with scrupulous, promptness and it should be made clear that there is to be no repudiation of them in any circumstances. Since the advantages of trade are continuous and also the advantages of cheap financing, this is expedient on the lowest grounds of self-interest, whatever views may be held in Socialist countries about the morality of meeting obligations incurred to capitalists.

Should a Socialist state also incur long-term debts abroad, if it can borrow there at a rate less than its own rate of interest at home? Since its own rate of interest represents its estimate of the marginal productivity of its own capital, it follows that there will be a net gain from borrowing abroad after interest and sinking-fund charges have been met: if the capital is properly employed, it will earn these and leave a surplus available to increase the consumption of goods at home. It follows that there is an advantage to be gained from such borrowing; even if it is expected that later there will be enough saving to lower the rate, a suitable arrangement of maturities will allow the loans to be paid off, the new savings taking the form of export surpluses. This will require careful adjustment of the industrial structure, since saving to take this form will require development different from that which would occur if the saving is in the form of new capital goods; but there is no theoretical difficulty.

From a practical point of view the question is not an easy one. It seems to be inexpedient to allow private capital to develop the country, as was tried at one time by Russia, since the success of the whole system depends on the possibility of unified control. The borrowing must be done by the state, and in order to take advantage of the lower rates available elsewhere strict guarantees would be necessary, which would hamper the political relations of the country. As has been remarked when dealing with new capital development, it is easy to make mistakes about the gain to be expected from expenditure of capital on a large scale; and when the saving required is to be done by others, the temptation to resort to borrowing to overcome temporary difficulties is great. The experience of borrowing by undeveloped countries in the past is not reassuring, and although the discussion of control in the whole of this book does not assume any particular level of competence on the part of the Ministry, there is an obvious difference between transactions entirely within its control and at the expense of the country as a whole, and those in which the citizens or the Governments of other countries are concerned. But in any case little can be said here of practical considerations, which are outside the scope of our discussion and which should only be treated empirically.

Transactions on capital account between two Socialist countries, though in a different category, are also beyond the range of our discussion. The question which would have to be decided before the terms were settled is the attitude of the one in which capital is most plentiful to the interests of the citizens of the other. The same question would arise in all dealings of an economic character between Socialist countries. We have been assuming so far that the economic advantages inside the country will be open to all, so that the equilibrium position will be one in which it is indifferent to the marginal individuals where they reside or in what occupation they are employed.

It is clearly not a matter of indifference to the individual whether he lives in an advanced or a backward country, economically speaking. The Communist party, who are at present the most active advocates of the kind of Socialism which we have been considering, have a strictly international outlook in matters of this kind, and appear to envisage perfect freedom of movement between countries. The logical development of this frame of mind would be to move the capital of all Socialist countries about until the rate of interest in all of them should be the same, and not to make any charge for capital sent from one country to another. It is arguable that the workers of an advanced country would object to the reduction of their standard of living which would follow from an influx of workers from less developed countries, or from an efflux of their own capital in an endeavour to equalise interest rates everywhere. Yet if it is considered that workers as a whole have a right to the accumulations of property and knowledge from the past, which accumulations are the main cause of the differences between economic development existing at present, it is difficult to see why one set of workers should be favoured rather than another because of the country in which they happen to live.

This problem has not yet received any accurate treatment in the writings of Socialists, though it is certainly one which will arise if any large part of the world should adopt Socialist forms of economic organisation. But in the absence of suitable hypotheses it is useless to attempt analysis.

APPENDIX

THE ECONOMIC SYSTEM
IN SOVIET RUSSIA

ALL theoretical work must be referred to practical experience for confirmation or refutation. Unfortunately the only experiment of Socialism on a large scale which has been made so far is that of Russia, which is still in a condition of change and transition. There have been several experiments in isolated communities, which have been unsuccessful. None of those had a developed price mechanism: in every case there were various circumstances besides this which might be adduced as reasons for the lack of success. But it will be of interest to examine the Russian system in the light of the analysis which has been made in the body of this work. The writer has not been to Russia and cannot read Russian, and can obviously make no claim to be either original or authoritative in the following account. But there are already many books and articles on the subject, and there is little disagreement about the main lines which have been followed.

The Russian economy is usually described as a planned system. This term is sometimes used of a price-controlled economy, but should be used for one in which the decisions are taken directly by the planning authority, which balances means and ends by one act of judgement, as an individual acting without economic relationships does. The Russians began in this way, being hardly guided at all by prices and costs in the sense in which we have used the terms: according to the Webbs, they have a profound contempt for the economists of Western countries, and they achieved a good deal with arrangements deliberately made, in which it was impossible to discover prices and costs at all in any economic sense. But the trend of the changes in recent years has been in the direction of a price system in which supply and demand are more in evidence. And although it would be rash to make any prophecies, it may be said that if the present trends continue they will develop an economic system not unlike the one which we have sketched above. It is no part of our inquiry to consider the extent to which they have solved their productive problem in the sense of attaining physical efficiency, but the opinions of those who have studied the matter are less unfavourable every year: and it would be gratifying if we should observe that this improvement coincided with the adoption of a price mechanism.

In the first place, there is no doubt that the state has complete control in economic matters. The independent producers, whose existence was sanctioned by the New Economic Policy, had practically disappeared by the end of 1932.[1] But there are still organisations which retain the appearance of independence. Farming is carried out, not only by state farms which are completely controlled, but by collective farms, which pay a tax of part of their produce to the state and are allowed to sell the remainder for the benefit of their members; and by individual peasants, who will presumably be organised in collective or state farms in the course of time. The distributive trades are organised in a variety of ways: shops directly controlled by the state, consumers' co-operatives which have some independence, and workers' supply departments attached to and controlled by the directors and personnel of the factories. In 1932 the consumers' co-operatives distributed 55 per cent of all goods destined for the consumers.[2] There is also something resembling an open market in the towns, in which the members of the collective farms and the independent peasants can sell their surplus produce direct to the consumers. The consumers' co-operatives are losing their importance, and in September 1935 the shops in the towns were transferred by decree to the Commissariat for Domestic Trade.[3] Production is carried out to some extent by the co-operative societies and by the workers' factory co-operatives, both of which produce goods such as milk and dairy products for consumption by their own members.[4] There are also co-operative societies of producers in the handicraft trades (the incops and artels), which control the production and sale of their own products: and finally there are individual workers, who can engage if they choose in such occupations as dressmaking and performing small services for householders.[5] The co-operative producers can even employ small percentages of wage workers, but they cannot restrict their membership, and they are forced to lower their prices if they do well enough to pay their members much above trade-union rates.[6] Theoretically these organisations allow of independent decisions and of differential gains to individuals from the ownership of property: practically they are of little significance. A factory might turn much of its energies to the supply of its own members, and an efficient co-operative society might do much better for its members than an inefficient one. But almost all these organisations have to submit their proposed proceedings for incorporation in the general plan, and they are closely controlled in all that they do, especially through the all-pervading influence of the Communist party.[7] There is no doubt that there is so much control in Russia as to justify us in calling it a Socialist state, and these examples of limited independence are either transitional or convenient forms of organisation. The freedom of individuals to do odd jobs and the organisation of handicraft co-operatives, for example, are methods of overcoming the difficulties which it has been suggested would be likely to arise when the productive unit is naturally small.

The control of production, however, is carried out only to a limited extent by the use of prices. The statistics which are published and the general form of the plans are given in terms of prices: Russian writers make constant reference to the control of processes with reference to prices and costs: but these do not yet mean what they do in ordinary economic language. A large proportion of all production (stated by Nodel as 44 per cent[8]) is distributed

directly for the service of other ends than those of
the citizens as consumers. This is done to some extent by all states, but to allow of calculation it is
necessary to make money grants and allow the state
departments to bid for what they require: in Russia
it is more the practice to allot goods directly though
their values are stated. When we come to the consumer, all observers agree that rationing is general[9]:
it is a crime to buy goods in order to resell them, a
proceeding which would not usually be profitable if
there were free markets. "The value of the rouble
varied with the holder."[10]

The reasons for which rationing was adopted are
not clear: the Webbs say frankly, "The determination of the particular ends to be attained . . . is the
business of the U.S.S.R. Government itself".[11] It
has also been suggested that the state wished to sell
goods at cost, which can only be done by rationing
if they are in short supply: and that there was an
original reluctance to make large differences in
money wages, so that the better or more favoured
workers were given better supplies directly.[12] In
the distribution of agricultural produce, the peasants
and collective farms sell some of their produce either
to co-operatives or to final consumers for what it
will fetch: some at low prices to co-operatives or to
factory shops, which they are induced to do by the
offer of manufactured goods which are obtained from
the state at low prices for this purpose: some is sold
to the state at a nominal price as a sort of tax. The
state exercises some sort of supervision over all these
prices, and indeed fixes prices at every turn. "In

carrying out this system of price fixing, the Government is guided partly by costs of production, partly by the relation of demand and supply, and partly by political and social considerations."[13] The co-operative and factory shops sell goods to their members at special low prices, partly in accordance with the status of the workers. Other goods are sold in the state shops to anyone who has the money: the prices are kept high enough to satisfy the demand, but as there are few purchases there, the open market must cover only a small part of the whole output.[14] It appears to be the intention of the authorities to abandon this system of rationing in the near future. Nodel in 1932 said, "within the next year or two, it will be possible to abandon the system of rationing and of closed shops".[15] His hopes were somewhat premature, but the most recent non-Russian writers observe that they are in process of realisation. "An open market for all consumers' goods is becoming the only channel of distribution. We can now estimate a price-level and compute values in terms of money."[16] "The trend is towards a system of unified prices."[17] We may say that most of the prices do not represent the relations of supply and demand, but that an increasing number are doing so.

Until this is general, the state cannot have any prices of finished goods in which it can place any confidence, and it is difficult to know in what units it can make its calculations, since its money is to a large extent meaningless (because of the variety of price-levels). The state may think it desirable that its members should get what it thinks good for them, and rationing is a possible method of discrimination, though it is perhaps easier to do this with money payments and a free market. But though it fixes the prices of finished goods and of producers' goods at all stages, these are only assertions of the relative validity of physical quantities of goods, and the assumptions made have to be carried over to the pricing of the factors of production. In the last analysis, the control of production in Russia has been through an immediate balance in the minds of those responsible for the plan: a superhuman task when we consider the complexity of the relevant data even in an economy with little variety either of products or of productive factors.

That it has been impossible to use prices as a guide to production in the past is clearly demonstrated by the fact that there have been several periods of currency inflation, especially to carry out expansions of capital during the First Five-Year Plan.[18] This destroys the basis of any calculations previously made, especially of the value of capital goods. The Webbs refer to "the whole decade" of experience behind the central planning organisation, but this cannot have been experience of price relationships. When expansion occurred, the money was made available to enterprises which it was considered desirable to enlarge: and after being paid out there, found its way to the workers for the purchase of goods. But it was a common experience for the workers to have money but nothing on which to spend it, a plain indication that the prices had no economic meaning.[19] The production must have been

239

controlled through an order of priority, an alternative method though perhaps lacking in delicacy of touch.

This is the essence of planning, as opposed to control through the price-cost relationship. Both the Five-Year Plans consisted of plans for producing quantities of goods which it was decided were necessary. When the general level of production is low, as it was in Russia, it is likely that the planning authority will want what the people want in the case of consumption goods: and in the case of capital goods the central authority has in any case to make the decisions. When the food ration is inadequate it cannot be far wrong to stimulate grain production: but when this point has been passed it will be possible to make goods which no-one will want, as appears to have happened in the case of books, "the only commodities of which in the U.S.S.R. the supply often exceeds the demand".[20] This is attributed to the lack of co-ordination between the producers and the public. With such planning there is no need to be concerned about the prices of productive factors, since the decision to make the goods involves the allocation of sufficient productive factors. Costing is mainly useful in such an economy as between units producing the same kind of goods: though if reliable figures of costs could be obtained, these would provide data which might be taken into account by the central authority in constructing the plan. This would involve a knowledge of the substitutability of the factors of production for one another at various margins.

240

"Gosplan obtains annually with regard to every enterprise in the U.S.S.R. . . . . an elaborate statistical statement as to what it has produced or done during the last completed year: what is going on during the current year; and what is expected during the year ensuing; including, in particular, how many workers of the various kinds and grades; and what amounts and kinds of materials and components have been or will be required; and what demands on the banking and transport services are involved." The consumers' co-operative reports how many people it has been supplying and how many it expects to supply: the kinds of commodities and their aggregate amounts: which it can produce for itself, which it will need to obtain from other U.S.S.R. producers, which it proposes to import. Corresponding data are obtained from the incops, the artels, and the collective farms: from transport and cultural institutions. Inspectors and instructors spur on the laggards. Thus a picture is formed of what would be done if the parts were free and able to do what they wanted. Simultaneously the Central Committee of the Communist Party will have been coming to general conclusions as to the particular expansions and new developments to be pressed forward. The whole aggregate must be brought into a very complicated balance.[21] But recently the co-ordinating or "synthetic" sections of Gosplan have been becoming of greater importance, and as the price system develops we should expect them to have more to do.[22]

The plan for the next year's production is then made and submitted for criticism to the organisations concerned: they make suggestions and emendations, and return the figures to the central body, which brings it into final adjustment. The co-ordination at the centre allows the whole of the productive resources and no more to be utilised: and brings the intentions of the Government into relation with the general scheme, which appears to be much more decided by the local than the central bodies. "If, for instance, a railway plan has to be prepared, the working out of this plan begins with the lowest links: their drafts are then referred to the administration of the particular railway, and lastly to the administrative authorities for railway transport as a whole."[23] Polanyi says that the planning of local enterprises by the central government has become almost a formality.[24]

The consumers are consulted mainly through the distributive bodies, which order what they find that their customers want, though this must be somewhat difficult when they cannot spend all their money. The wholesale trade is carried out by industrial organisations, which are "easily able to appreciate changes in the demand and adapt (themselves) to them without delay".[25] The whole process is fairly simple so long as not too much variety is produced: there is a rough adaptation to the wants of the consumers also when local bodies submit schemes for producing what they want themselves. But with the directing consciousness shared among the Government, the planning authorities at the centre, and the productive organisations at the periphery, it seems doubtful whether there is any accurate balancing of means and ends: which would require immediate knowledge on the part of all these bodies, not only of final values but also of the alternative capacities of resources. We are not concerned with the actual results, about which there is naturally a considerable difference of opinion. But criticisms may be quoted which indicate possible economic difficulties. "As a condition of its [the Five-Year Plan's] fulfilment, it assumed the highest quality of labour."[26] "It offers truly enormous scope for red tape and bureaucratic inefficiency."[27] "Any production exceeding the plan is acclaimed as a victory and is regarded as an offset to other productions falling short of the plan."[28] "The Bolshevik planners seem to have very little conception of demand *at a price*, but regard it as something absolute."[29] It should be remembered that the most important task in Russia so far has been to extend production in almost any direction; owing to the low level of efficiency, almost any goods were likely to be advantageous, if not the most advantageous possible, and it was of great importance to be sure that when production was called for the resources would respond. Some sacrifice in the nice adjustment of means and ends is justified in the interests of physical efficiency which will give even a rude plenty. But when there is more confidence in the level of output the situation will change. "As the number of factories increase, as industry becomes diversified, as the possibilities of consumers' choice become greater, the problems confronting the Soviet planners become more complex."[30]

The construction of new capital goods is part of

the plan: it is decided that new capacity is required without more ado. This may also be done because it appears that it will be profitable in the monetary sense, but since the prices, and, as we shall see, the costs, are not a reliable guide, central decisions about the direction in which savings are to materialise are at least as reasonable as the use of the concept of profitability. New capital construction is carried out partly from taxes, partly from loans, partly from the differences between receipts and costs of state enterprises, and partly from inflation. As we have seen, the decision as to how much to save cannot be made by the Socialist state on any but general grounds. But if there were a reliable price system, it could be used to decide the form in which savings were to materialise.

When the final prices are not representative of any particular supply-demand relationship, costs cannot be imputed from them. For an authoritative plan which calls for fixed quantities of each good to be produced precludes us from making comparisons of productive resources in different lines of production: each is essential up to the amount required and almost useless after that point, so that even when they are physically substitutable for one another they cannot strictly be compared: there are not degrees of indispensability. And to allow excesses in one line to balance deficiencies elsewhere seems to be abandoning even the plan. No doubt the relative quantities of factors required for each kind of production are taken into consideration when the plan is made: some preference is given to what is easy to produce: but the calculation is an immediate one like that of an individual weighing up different uses of his time rather than a mathematical balancing. The Russians have figures of costs: but they must be of an arbitrary character and only useful in ensuring efficient production of each separate commodity. They do not regard profits as a reason for expansion nor losses as a reason for contracting,[31] and this is quite reasonable when the costs and the prices are unreliable.[32]

There is great stress in the works of Russian writers on the importance of cost accounting, but this cannot be of much use except as a guide towards checking waste and improving output in each separate line of production. If the figures called for in the plan are taken as final, it is possible to get some adjustments with arbitrary figures of costs. The trusts which control the productive units fix an average cost of production at the existing cost figures for an efficient works, and reward those units which get below this, while making inquiries when it is exceeded. This should lead the directors of factories, farms, and other units gradually to substitute cheaper for dearer factors until they arrive at the cheapest methods of production for the cost figures given: while the low-cost production can be expanded and the high-cost contracted. This should then lead to a shortage of some factors and a surplus of others, which might be followed both by a modification of the plan (producing more of goods which can be made by the surplus factors), and by an alteration of the cost figures. The only problem then remaining would be the relation between the cost figures and the specific productivity of each factor: this must be assumed to be satisfactory from the fact that the quantities produced are those required by the plan. But it seems very unlikely that much progress has been made in this direction, or even that there is much intention of making it at present. This can be seen from a consideration of the method of fixing costs.

These can be reduced to two main heads: labour costs and a tax for capital expansion and for Government purposes. It does not appear that either interest as such, or rent, is considered an important cost. The productive units have to pay for the intermediate goods which they use, but the prices of these in turn are made up of the same two costs, and the plan stipulates the prices at which the products are to be transferred at every stage. The total wage bill is fixed for each year by negotiation between the Trade Union representatives and representatives of the directors and managers of the industrial units, the principal consideration being the amount of goods available. "The statistics worked out by the State Planning Commission carry irresistible weight."[33] It is difficult to know how the Planning Commission gets its statistics: the inference from the Webbs is that the total wage bill is regulated by the expected quantities and prices of goods which are to be available for the workers, but with so much rationing this seems impossible. It might also be done from the expected outgoings of the industries, but this is a circular method. In any case, *some* sum is agreed: and it is then distributed according to a common system of grading.[34] Piece-work is the basic system of remuneration, as we might expect from Stalin's principle, "To each according to his work". The grading system is designed to encourage workers to enter occupations in which there is a scarcity of labour.[35] This is decided by what is called "social value", and is settled from the requirements of the plan: so that we may say that labour costs represent the productive value of labour in the eyes of the State Planning Commission. Since the order of production has been settled already, this is not yet of much consequence: but differential payments are used in all price economies to attract supplies of labour which are considered to be scarce.

On the collective farms payment is chiefly in kind and there are no real pricing arrangements. After the deduction of the state contributions, the balance is divided among the workers in accordance with the amount of work done individually. The unit of computation is the "working day", the number of these contained in a job varying with the job as well as the intensity of work.[36] The return to the peasants does not seem to compare with the return to industrial work.

There is some difference of opinion among the writers who have described the Russian economy about the use of interest as a cost. The Russians who describe parts of the system in the series published by Gollancz do not mention it at all, from which we may conclude that it is not a usual cost. Neither Mrs. Wootton nor the Webbs think it is common, and

Hoover says that "as important economic categories, both rent and interest have disappeared". Feiler says, "No provision is made for interest upon the credits to which the business has resorted, and which are, in fact, often granted free of interest".[37] All these writers appear to be thinking about interest on the fixed capital: advances for capital construction are made by the banks for long-term capital and, as far as I have been able to find, no interest is charged on these.[38] But interest *is* charged on working or circulating capital: Hoover says that it is charged according to the profitability of the industry to which the loans are made,[39] and Burns in an analysis of costs includes a small amount for interest. The best account I have found is contained in monographs of the London University School of Slavonic Studies, which contain the statement, "Interest on all forms of credit is usually at 6 per cent per annum". As Gosbank gets its revenue from the interest it charges, it is clear that it must make some charge: but this is not arrived at through relating supply and demand.

The use of long-term capital does, however, involve a cost, for all industries have to provide for their own depreciation and for funds for the general expansion of industry. Hoover gives the allowance for depreciation as an average of 6½ per cent.[40] In addition the state fixes the prices of intermediate goods in order to allow reasonably efficient works to make a profit and itself makes a first charge on this profit.[41] Even if this were not done, the neglect of interest would not have the effect it would have in a capitalist state of over-expanding the capital-using industries, since expansion is not based on profitability: indeed it would be truer to say that the state decides where to expand and then fixes the prices and costs so that production will be profitable.[42] Interest, then, is treated even less than wages in the way suggested in this book.

Where the book results depend on the central policy, there cannot be any systematic use of the concept of rent. As between enterprises producing similar goods, it could be used along with the concept of profit in order to discover whether low profits were due to inefficiency or to poor resources. There is "socialist" competition between such enterprises, and Reddaway says that each productive unit is rated according to its efficiency when the control figures are fixed: it meets its costs from its receipts, and, being forced to pay to the state by its rating, has in effect to meet a rent charge. This seems to be another example of the gradual introduction of a pricing mechanism. Nodel says that the tax which has to be paid by the collective farms is assessed according to the fertility of the soil. They have to pay heavily for the use of tractors and the payment is a proportion of the crop.[43] No rent is paid for the allotments used by individuals or co-operatives for growing their own food-stuffs,[44] and the rent of houses "is only just barely sufficient to pay for the necessary repairs and other expenses in connection with maintenance".[45]

On the whole, then, it seems unlikely that the costs at present can be reliable indices. They serve to control the operations of the directors of industry, but do not really measure the alternative possibilities of the productive resources. Yet the Russians must be becoming accustomed to the use of them, and as the open market supersedes the closed shops it will be possible gradually to expand or to contract production in various directions until the amount demanded at the fixed cost is equal to the amount produced. When this stage is reached, it will be possible to introduce further refinements: in particular it will be necessary at some stage to allow the various branches to compete for resources. There seem to be some dangers in treating labour costs as the amount actually paid to the workers, though this is an immense convenience. It is dangerous to dogmatise in the absence of information about the principles which actuate the "synthetic" sections of Gosplan: but I think that the costs follow from, rather than precede, their decisions.

"The director of a factory has supreme authority in the conduct of the daily activity of his enterprise and is personally responsible for its success or failure."[46] It is generally agreed that there is little unemployment. On the other hand, it is probably more difficult to live without working in Russia than in many Western countries: "He who does not work, neither shall he eat". This maxim would cause some outcry in England. With such complete control over the economic system, it would be a severe criticism of the government if there were involuntary employment on a large scale such as we find in capitalist countries.

The system of money and banking is described by
several writers. "The Russians have not troubled to
formulate any reasoned monetary policy."[47] The
gold standard was abandoned early in the process of
development, and notes are now issued by the State
Bank and the Commissariat of Finance. There are
two banks, the Gosbank and the Prombank, for
short- and long-term credits to industry respectively:
and also a co-operative bank and an agricultural
bank. Presumably their operations are all controlled
according to a central plan. Inter-industry transactions are carried out with credit, but since the
industries are expected to pay their own workers
from their receipts, the circulating money cannot
be kept distinct from bank money. There has been
a good deal of inflation in order to provide capital
for carrying out the Five-Year Plan. But owing to
the fixing of prices, this does not cause them to rise
very much, leading rather to queues.[48] And the
Government gets the money back again by means of
loans, "subscription to which is practically compulsory".[49] The same result would have been achieved
by lowering money wages: in any case the workers
cannot get more goods for consumption than are
produced. It seems somewhat unnecessary to go to
the trouble of inflating, regulating prices and taking
off the available money by forced loans or by charging very high prices for the few unrationed goods.
No doubt questions of prestige or doctrine were involved. But here again changes are taking place:
there has been little inflation since 1932,[50] and as
the free shops extend, these and amusements are

taking off the available purchasing power.[51]

The bank credit is made available for each productive unit according to the central plan. "Regulating credit does not mean fixing a total volume for which individual enterprises may bid, but in drawing up an elaborate credit plan which ultimately lays down how much each enterprise may borrow and even for what purpose."[52] "The planning organs are now (1931) supposed to proceed upon the assumption that the necessary money will be provided for any project if the physical factors essential to its success can be provided by the Soviet economy."[53] On ordinary lines this would lead to great disturbances of the price mechanism: but when production is regulated by specific directions it is of little consequence how it is financed. Indeed the danger would be that the Russians might allow themselves to be influenced by their prices and costs under the impression that these had some validity. Hoover, writing of the rouble of 1930, said that "it still serves with reasonable efficiency as a book-keeping standard of value", but subsequently it can only have been a very rough guide.[54]

The state has a monopoly of foreign trade, and carries it out in terms of foreign currency.[55] "The Soviet Government is compelled by this system to regulate its purchases abroad so that the supplies of foreign valuta which it receives from the sale of commodities in foreign markets are always adequate to pay for current purchases or to meet obligations which fall due on account of goods which have been bought on short-term credit."[56] A number of writers

APPENDIX

on Russia seem to think that the problem of foreign trade is a difficult one. Hoover says that the problem of the relation between the internal and external value of the rouble is frequently discussed by Soviet economists.[57] But there need be no particular relation, given the peculiar nature of costs in Russia: no exchange rate could have much significance. "In general the organisation of Russian foreign trade makes it possible for goods which are extremely scarce at home to be exported."[58] "It is an anxious problem to decide which commodities it will be most profitable or least costly to the U.S.S.R. to produce in order to ship to foreign countries."[59] These anxieties seem unjustified:[60] they have exported whatever they could find a market for abroad[61] in order to get machinery and raw materials which were high in their order of urgency and which in most cases they could hardly have made for themselves at all. It is probable that they have not yet reached the point of accurate adjustment, but are at the top and bottom of the comparative cost scales, exporting commodities such as timber produced mainly by unskilled labour, and importing things which they could not produce and on which they set a high value, so that the gain is enormous. The balance which has to be struck is one of direct utilities rather than of comparative costs: at what point is current consumption so much reduced as to make the loss of satisfaction from further reduction equivalent in the eyes of the authorities to the further gain which would result from quickening the tempo of industrialisation through further imports? There will only be a cost problem when imports are for current consumption: at this stage it would become advantageous to know what rate of interest represents the productivity of capital in terms of other factors. The Russians may console themselves for any economic shortcomings they may have in their conduct of foreign trade by a contemplation of the methods by which it is conducted elsewhere. Feiler says that they have a tariff[62] but this cannot be of any significance when all trade is controlled: it appears to have been used to increase the accounting prices of imported goods, in order to restrict their use industrially: a sort of index of the urgency of the demand for foreign exchange generally.

They have attempted to borrow abroad, because the gain, in the opinion of the planning authorities, from the goods which might thus be bought would far outweigh the cost of the annual payments: their rate of interest in the sense of their demand for capital is high, although they do not know what it is. But they have obtained little but short-term credits for obvious reasons: and in their nature these can only be of limited amount.

New developments appear to be encouraged: where they replace existing methods there can be a direct comparison of resources involved, though it is difficult to see how an invention would be judged which called for capital but saved labour. The Russians certainly cannot be accused of stagnating, and the accounts of some of their large projects are impressive. Neither they nor anyone else could at present say whether they put their capital to the most productive use in a measurable sense: this uncertainty is involved in the planning method. "Whoever discovers an improvement is supposed to make it immediately available to others . . . but difficulties are continuously encountered when it is sought to put this principle into operation."[63]

It will be seen from this account that the Russians trust principally to the wisdom and the good intentions of the central controlling body: planning does not mean the careful adjustment of means to ends, but the subordination of the economic body to a central will which forms immediate judgements without the use of the monetary balance. There can be little doubt that this causes what would be considered fairly large losses of welfare in price economies, both through the production of goods which are not wanted so much as others would have been if the consumers had a free choice: and through the lack of knowledge about the relative costs of productive resources. There are reasons for supposing that they are making a greater use of prices now than they have done in the past. And they seem to be able to impart an energy to their members which may compensate in output for the loss of economic values. We may agree with a severe critic of planning when he says, "Every Government may make mistakes in its economic policy: only the planned economy bestows upon the Government so much power that such mistakes may develop into catastrophes and yet hardly endanger the position of the Government".[64] It is true that they may: but there is little reason why they should.

NOTES TO APPENDIX

[1] W. Nodel, *Supply and Trade in the U.S.S.R.*, p. 29.
[2] Nodel, p. 30. See also S. and B. Webb, *Soviet Communism: A New Civilisation?* p. 333.
[3] Lorwin and Abramson, *International Labour Review*, Jan. 1936, p. 13.
[4] *E.g.* Nodel, ch. x.
[5] Webbs, p. 721. Also in ch. iii. sect. 2.
[6] Webbs, pp. 227 *et seq.*
[7] Nodel, p. 83. Cf. E. Burns, *Russia's Productive System*, p. 114.
[8] Nodel, p. 12. This is an under-estimate. L. E. Hubbard, *Soviet Money and Finance*, says "only about one-third of the national income was in consumable form" [in 1933], p. 191.
[9] *E.g.* Webbs, p. 324; W. Reddaway, *The Russian Financial System*, p. 5. See also Tverskoi, *The Unified Transport System of the U.S.S.R.*, pp. 23, 24; Calvin B. Hoover, *The Economic Life of Soviet Russia*, pp. 8, 208, 253.
[10] Lorwin and Abramson, p. 19.
[11] Webbs, p. 631.
[12] Nodel, ch. vi., is very frank about the preferential treatment of particular grades of workers when they buy.
[13] Lorwin and Abramson, p. 15.
[14] Reddaway, p. 44; Nodel, pp. 63, 88; Webbs, p. 733; B. Brutskus, *Economic Planning in Soviet Russia*, p. 148.
[15] Nodel, p. 62.
[16] M. Polanyi, *U.S.S.R. Economics* (Manchester University Press), p. 3.
[17] Lorwin and Abramson, p. 15. See also Monograph 9 of the School of Slavonic Studies, *The End of Rationing and the Standard of Living in the Soviet Union.*
[18] See especially Brutskus, pp. 144 *et seq.*; Hoover, ch. viii.
[19] See, *e.g.*, Reddaway, p. 74; Webbs, p. 324, who attribute this to the "growth in effective demand, with which it is impossible to keep pace". This is a common phenomenon in inflations, not peculiar to Russia.

APPENDIX

20 Marc Jaryĉ, *Press and Publishing in the Soviet Union* (Monograph 6 of the School of Slavonic Studies in the University of London), p. 22.

21 Quotation and Summary from the Webbs, pp. 626 *et seq.*, who give an admirable description of the process. Most writers stress the planning from the bottom upwards.

22 Lorwin and Abramson, p. 31.

23 Tverskoi, p. 25. He ends this chapter, "The fact that the transport plan is known among all transport workers *guarantees* its successful working" (my italics).

24 Polanyi, p. 18.

25 Nodel, p. 41.

26 Brutskus, p. 137.

27 Reddaway, p. 35. He is discussing the control of credit, but the remark is applicable to the whole system.

28 Polanyi, p. 15.

29 Lorwin and Abramson, p. 33.

30 Reddaway, p. 84.

31 *E.g.* B. Wootton, *Plan or No Plan*, p. 70; Hoover, p. 24; Tverskoi, pp. 21, 22.

32 Mrs. Wootton (*op. cit.* p. 91) gives a striking example of the paper profits possible in a planned economy, in her example of children making important electrical apparatus at a profit.

33 Webbs, pp. 185 *et seq.*

34 Webbs, pp. 186 *et seq.*

35 Hoover, p. 256; Wootton, pp. 77 *et seq.*; Webbs, p. 186.

36 Lorwin and Abramson, for piece-work generally.

37 A. Feiler, *The Experiment of Bolshevism*, English Trans., p. 105.

38 M. Dobb, *Russian Economic Development*, p. 180; Monographs 4 and 5 of the School of Slavonic Studies, *Banking and Credit in the U.S.S.R.*, p. 56.

39 Hoover, p. 190.

40 Hoover, p. 26.

41 See Monographs on *Banking and Credit in the U.S.S.R.*

42 All works on Russian economics emphasise the fact that profitability is not the test for capital expansion; *e.g.* Reddaway, "Supplementary grants are freely made where funds are wasted", p. 41. The co-operatives which

257

make high profits are prosecuted: with rationing this seems almost necessary.

[43] Kunitz, *Dawn over Samarkand*, p. 209. Cf. Webbs, p. 253.

[44] Nodel, p. 154.

[45] Hoover, p. 255.

[46] Lorwin and Abramson, p. 20.

[47] Wootton, p. 210.

[48] Hoover, p. 209. The Webbs do not think the queues of much significance, and this is confirmed by the most recent writers.

[49] Hoover, p. 251. See Brutskus, *passim*, for the inflationary tendencies.

[50] Monograph of the School of Slavonic Studies, 4.

[51] Monographs, 4 and 5, p. 73.

[52] Reddaway, p. 17.

[53] Hoover, p. 217.

[54] Cf. Monograph 3, "there are a number of widely differing price-levels in operation in the Soviet Union", p. 17.

[55] J. D. Yanson, *Foreign Trade in the U.S.S.R.*, pp. 23, 25.

[56] Hoover, p. 219.

[57] Hoover, p. 222.

[58] Brutskus, p. 151.

[59] Webbs, p. 630.

[60] Yanson is more sensible than foreigners who discuss the system—he writes a whole book on foreign trade without discussing the price policy.

[61] See Yanson, pp. 29, 83, 93, on the difficulties of getting markets.

[62] Feiler, p. 107. *Cf.* Hoover, p. 155.

[63] Feiler, p. 108.

[64] Brutskus, p. 232.

Note on Bibliography.—There are many books on Russian economics, usually containing critical accounts of the actual results. Those of Hoover and Mrs. Wootton are very good, though like all books on Russia they become more out of date each year. The great work by Mr. and Mrs. Webb should be read by all who are interested in Russia generally, though their economic views are not orthodox in many places. I have used writers favourable to the Russian experiment

APPENDIX

wherever possible, since my conclusion, that they do not make much use of a price system in my sense, is most convincing when supported by their own writers. It would be possible to confirm this outline from other works not cited. See in particular L. E. Hubbard, *Soviet Money and Finance*, for changes following the removal of rationing; and Alexander Gourvitch, "The Problem of Prices and Valuation in the Soviet System", *American Economic Review*, March 1936, Supplement.

INDEX

INDEX

THE END

SC   SCIENCE